8 MOMENTS
OF POWER
IN COACHING

8 MOMENTS
OF POWER
IN COACHING

HOW TO **DESIGN** AND **DELIVER** HIGH-PERFORMANCE
FEEDBACK TO ALL EMPLOYEES

MARK COLGATE, Ph.D.

elevate

Copyright © 2016 by Mark Colgate

Editorial work by AnnaMarie McHargue
Interior design by Kiran Spees
Cover design by Aaron Snethen
Cover photography by Jared Erondu, www.Unsplash.com

Published in Boise, Idaho by Elevate, an imprint of Elevate Publishing

This book may be purchased in bulk for educational, business, organizational, or promotional use.

For information, please email info@elevatepub.com

Hardback ISBN-13: 9781943425853
eBook ISBN-13: 9781943425860

Library of Congress Control Number: 2016942442

Printed in the United States of America

To Orla, thank you for the thousands of fun, loving, and powerful moments we have had together…for sure, the most powerful moment of all was September 1988, when we were both just five.

Contents

Acknowledgments

It's always strange to me that authors acknowledge family last in their acknowledgments. For me, they must come first. Beyond the dedication, I wish to acknowledge Nesha, Callum, and Kian. We have had so many discussions around the table about this book and I'm very sorry, Callum, that I did not call this book "*Mark Colgate's ways to earn cash, cash, money, money.*" Yes, the title would have sold more, but a picture of me on the cover in the bath with lots of dollar bills, a gold chain around my neck, backwards cap, and lots of golden rings is just disturbing. I adore my friendship with all three of you, more than you will ever know.

To Mum, Dawn, Peter, and Paul, the effort you have put into our family and friendship is incredible. I may be far away, but I feel so close to you all. You inspire me and make me laugh so much; I thank you four from the bottom of my heart for all you have done for me.

In terms of professional friendships, Andrew Turner has been mind-blowing. Who could have known what we would achieve together? Professionally, no one has believed in me more; thank you so, so much. You even put so much effort into getting this book cover right—that's how amazing you are.

Barbara Chapman, my boss at Commonwealth Bank, was also my mentor, my coach, motivation, and my role model. You took a chance on me, and I hope I made you proud. When a boss makes you want to make *them* shine, rather than yourself, you know you have met someone special.

A special call out to my other amazing *leader coach*, you showed me what it means to lead with integrity and passion; Saul Klein, you are truly a servant leader.

In terms of the book, Anna McHargue was the perfect editor. Can an editor really make such a difference to a book? Yes, they really can. Incredibly reliable (her advice and knowledge), amazingly responsive (the fastest turnaround times you could imagine), and so much fun to work with (inspired me, encouraged me, and laughed with me). Mark Russell, a huge thanks to you as well for taking me on this journey, and a huge round of applause to the amazing Elevate team.

In terms of the case studies in this book, Felicity Barrenger, Toni Roberts, Stephanie Rule, Marlena Stubbings, Tim Johnston, Eddie Dryer, Robert MacKay, Marius Marginean, Russ Wood, Jeanne Biddulph, Jeff Puritt, and Andrew Martin were all so kind to give up their time for this book—a huge thank you!

Dan Pontefract, thank you, not only for the TELUS case study, but also for influencing me to write this book. You showed me what's possible if you have the right ideas, passion, and willingness to get it done. There are very few like you!

To Orla, who read so many parts of this book, and then, at the bitter end, all eight chapters one more time! Your ideas and insights were invaluable—I appreciate it all so much xxxxx.

To Val Litwin (the maker of the irresistible Litwin sauce) and Mecki Facundo (the most wonderful learning guru out there), you two are a dream team, a very special partnership that has just begun!

Finally, to all those astonishing people who have inspired me in so many ways, Heather Ranson (who taught the first coaching course with me many years ago and very kindly passed off some the resources in this book to me), Rupert Knight, Sudhir and Radhika Nair, Dean Duthie (I loved all our coaching coffees), Bodo Lang, Tessa Price, Denise LaMarche, Jeff Mallett, Louise Roberts, Erin Beattie, Lloyd Daser, and Brett and Jeanne Merriman, thank you.

And to all those Derby County fans out there—COYR!

Introduction

Rapunzel, Rapunzel, Let Down Your Guard

I have a wonderful story of someone whose life changed dramatically, all because of the power of coaching. Their productivity soared and, in a few short months, they got their dream promotion, a giant pay raise, unlimited admiration and…

Ha-ha, fooled you. That's not coaching, that's fairytale silliness. Coaching is about consistency, authenticity, and the long haul. It's about the coach and coachee working it out together. It's about alignment, feedback, and realizing that coaching is for everyone—not just executives.

Coaching is about being armed with data, growing the coachee's sense of accountability, and the coach playing the role of *head coach*; they can't provide high-quality feedback on everything. It's about the coach believing in the power of coaching and believing in the coachee, but not believing the hype about coaching. Coaching is hard. Being a coachee can be harder.

This book is about always turning up, even when you have doubts or are not seeing progress. This book is about energy—creating drive and momentum through coaching, but also creating vitality by helping coachees be in the best physical shape possible. Employees who have energy are great employees.

I don't have a rags-to-riches story for you, but what I do have is better. Unless, of course, you are looking for a fantasy bedtime story because my book is rubbish compared to one of those.

Defining Coaching

Are you crazy? I'm not going to define coaching. Ask 10 different people and you will get 10 different answers as to what coaching is. For me to create a definition of coaching that I insist you adopt is tedious (and ridiculous). You won't remember it, and you will like your definition better than mine.

All I need to tell you is the kind of coaching that this book encourages and lays out. If you buy into this approach, I think you will find your coaching to be better off. If not, then I will kidnap your youngest child and force them to listen to all the speeches Donald Trump has ever made. Good, we are all together then.

I encourage a particular type of coaching—one that I have seen work. One I wholeheartedly believe in. And, of course, one I simply don't think exists out there so far—otherwise I would not have written this book. The coaching I endorse has five parts:

1. It is designed as part of a system within an organization, so it feeds off and integrates with everything else that is going on (hiring, organization strategy, performance reviews, etc.).

2. It is based on carefully understanding human behavior. Managing the psychological context is critical to coaching. What you do before the coaching session may be more important than the coaching itself.

3. It is based on feedback. We live in a feedback-free society, where we find it hard to find the time to assist each other by offering or receiving high-quality feedback. This book, more than anything else, is about using coaching as a tool to create ongoing, high-quality feedback so we can grow. It's almost as simple as that.

4. I said almost! Coaching in this book takes a very specific *athletic approach to coaching*. This book espouses using three well-established parts to athletic coaching: technical coaching, mental coaching, and physical coaching. Great athletic coaches tap into all three parts. Athletic coaches create high-performing athletes, and we want to create high-performing employees. This book outlines what this looks like from an organizational context.

5. Finally, this book adopts a measurement perspective to coaching. We must measure the outcomes from coaching, so we know we are creating

high-performing employees. If we don't measure whether coaching is working or not, we could well be wasting our time.

And that's it—like *my* definition? Thought not, have it your way then, stick with your own. By the way, has anyone ever said you are childish?

Me!

My therapist said, "From my perspective, one problem you have is that you are so egocentric."

I said, "Enough of your perspective, let's talk about mine." Some of this comment from my therapist can be explained by the fact that I was raised as an only child, which really upset my sister and two brothers. Regardless of my own personal coaching needs, there are three reasons I believe this book will help you:

1. Most importantly, seeing is believing. I was incredibly fortunate to work for three years at one of the best organizations in the world. During my time at Commonwealth Bank of Australia, I saw the overwhelming power of coaching *all employees across the organization.* I also took the opportunity to become a coach to many frontline employees and learned first-hand the significance of adopting an athletic approach to coaching, which is the angle this book takes, as stated above.

2. I'm also very fortunate to work as a professor at the University of Victoria, Gustavson School of Business. What's so special about this business school? We are unique in that we are relatively small (about 50 professors), but we do not embrace a silo mentality, and do not departmentalize into finance, accounting, human resources, marketing, strategy, operations, and so forth. We all are part of one business school. On one side of me, I have an operations professor, on the other side, an international business professor, and down the corridor, there is an information systems professor, strategy professor, a guru on leadership, and so on.

    Over the last 10 years, this has enabled me to see business from so many different angles and put together many of the pieces that need to be considered in coaching. Coaching is about leadership. Coaching is about being a more productive organization so you are using your resources carefully. Coaching is a strategic choice. You either choose to coach across the organization, or you choose not to (which is fine, too, because it's better to choose not to do it, than to do it half-heartedly). Coaching is about managing employees. Coaching is marketing; effective coaching simultaneously increases employee engagement and customer engagement by motivating employees to raise the bar in terms of their skill levels—which will concurrently raise the customer experience (whether this is an internal or external customer) through a more potent collaboration with an employee.

I would argue that this is my strength. I have integrated many different organizational perspectives, which are all critical to coaching success. Taking a narrow point of view (for example, believing coaching is really a human resource activity, or that coaching is only for leaders) is a mistake, and likely means you will miss many opportunities to align coaching with everything else that goes on inside the organization.

3. Another asset of this book (mainly because I'm in a business school that has no departments) is that it covers such a vast array of interconnected concepts, all of which are fundamental to executing an effective approach to coaching across the organization. In essence, this book taps into eight main areas:

    a. Implicit personal theories: Often called fixed and growth mindsets, this research looks at how we view intelligence and natural-born talent. This book takes the growth mindset approach, meaning that it is coaching, not natural-born talent, which leads to high performance.

    b. Systems theory: To have a successful coaching approach in the organization, you need to take a systems view of coaching. You need to develop a system for coaching and embed coaching across the system in which the organization exists; otherwise coaching will not be sustainable.

    c. Behavioral science: There is an incredibly important and growing area of thought about how people behave. Driven by leading scholars such as Robert Cialdini, Daniel Kahnemam, and Steve Peters, this behavioral science teaches that if we are to truly understand how coaching can be successful in an organization, we must understand how people behave and the psychological context in which we coach employees.

Ignoring human behavior and expecting people to quickly adopt coaching is likely to lead to failure.

d. Expertise theory: Ultimately, coaching is about creating experts inside the organization. The goal of every organization must be to create high-performing experts who are always trying to improve. Fortunately, there is a significant science behind growing people's expertise and the three dimensions of expertise. We look at these three discoveries closely to ensure coaching is continuously focused on these dimensions.

e. Employee engagement: By growing the skills of employees through coaching, we have a chance to engage them so that they are motivated at work every single day. When the coach sits down with an employee and is authentic, believes in them, and helps them grow, then the employee will be more engaged. We tap into the science of employee engagement to show how coaching, if used carefully, can tap into this science.

f. Athletic coaching: Athletic coaching has a 100-year history. It is science that has been refined continuously and offers many opportunities for organizations to adapt and adopt some of its most successful techniques (such as observation and demonstration). We look at what is successful athletic coaching and the opportunities for organizations to adopt a more athletic approach to coaching inside their organization.

g. Fair process: Over the last few years there has been research conducted as to how to execute a "fair process" methodology inside an organization. Many organizations have successfully adopted this approach. Fair process is about realizing that the process is as important as the outcome (for example, the decision-making process is as important as the decision you make, if you want people to buy into it). We adopt a fair process model for coaching, and we show how fair process is a great way to sustainably execute coaching inside an organization.

h. Measurement: For coaching to be a success, it must be able to show that employees have learned from it and changed their behavior in a way that leads to positive organizational results. If we continue coaching without understanding whether the employees are getting anything out of the experience, whether they are willing to make changes based on coaching, and whether they actually have made progress based on coaching, then coaching will fail. Any time you coach, you're giving up time to be doing something else. It must be possible to show coaching is a success or we will lose faith in coaching and so will organizational leaders. We tap into the discipline of measurement to demonstrate how we can show whether coaching is making a difference or not.

These are the book's promises. I also promise I won't talk about myself again, except perhaps, at the beginning of the first chapter, and then chapters two through eight.

Moment of Power 1:
The Moment You Realize the Power of Coaching

I remember a day when I was 17, and I was sitting in a high school class with Mr. Thompson, my utterly brilliant history teacher.

Mr. Thompson was an Oxford University-educated teacher. Let me tell you, when you are taught at Oxford University, you not only learn history, but you also learn how to look like a historian. Mr. Thompson had a large black beard, (which cleverly represented the era in which he was teaching), leather patches on the elbows of his cardigan, flowing black cape, and a large cutlass in case we got rowdy.

One day in his class, in full historian outfit, Mr. Thompson was discussing the merits of sources of data and research credibility.

He then said something that stayed with me ever since, "The best discoveries in life are the ones you unearth when you were not looking for them in the first place." I remember this making an impact on me at the time, but it has become more meaningful to me over the years, as I've discovered the power of confirmation bias—our tendency to search for (and interpret) information in a way that confirms our original preconceptions. In the context of history, the teacher was referring to the habit of reading books or research articles that would reinforce the angle we were taking in the history essays we were writing. But, of course, this bias pervades every area of our lives.

Fast forward 20 years. As the General Manager of Customer Satisfaction at Commonwealth Bank of Australia, the power of being a coach (and being coached) would emerge—as a complete revelation to me—as one of the prevailing drivers in taking Commonwealth Bank from being the lowest performing major bank in Australia, in terms of customer service, to the very best, in the space of five years (at the time of this writing, Commonwealth Bank has been number one in customer satisfaction for four years in a row).

The genesis of the story is surprising given I am a professor, but ended up working in a real job with real working hours. You see, professors don't go out very much; we tend to shuffle between our offices and the classes that we teach, with only the occasional, uncomfortable contact with the outside world, and we certainly do not savor the idea of practicing what we preach. As a business professor, this means working in real business with real people.

Professors also lead a relatively relaxed lifestyle (in at 10 a.m., home by lunch). So much so, in fact, that when people ask me how many professors work at my university, my reply is generally, "Half of them." So, it was with deep trepidation that, in 2007, I left the University of Victoria—with permission to take a three-year leave of absence—to become a General Manager at Commonwealth Bank, the 10th largest bank in the world, to assist Commonwealth Bank reach its goal of being the very best in customer service.

Of course, I took my toolkit with me (given that helping organizations achieve their goals of service excellence is my main research and consulting area), and I helped out wherever I could in my three years there. However, there were two things Commonwealth Bank had decided to invest in already that had a far greater impact on achieving service excellence than any impact I personally had.

One of those two things was what they called *Sports Coaching*. (I will keep the other to myself, as my uncle taught me to always keep your customers wanting more. However, it's not always the best advice, as that's how he lost his job at the food bank.) This meant that every single employee was mandated to get 30 minutes of *observational*-based coaching every week. Yes, every week! Some of you are immediately thinking, as I was, how could the leaders possibly afford the time to coach each team member every single week?

As it turns out, the answer from these leaders, when I posed this question, was frequently, "How can I afford not to find the time?" (Although, to be honest, they may have known I was coming.)

So, for example, in the bank branches the team leader would observe an employee, watch some of their real-time customer interactions, and then do a post hoc coaching session based on the interactions they just observed. The impact of this coaching on employee engagement and the ability of the employees to increase their skills in their domain of expertise was incredible. In fact, it was something I never expected.

In addition to seeing the impact coaching made, there was also a natural control group since some leaders executed the mandate of sports coaching much better than others, in that they turned up more frequently, they were more authentic, and they integrated the coaching into the other practices the bank required (e.g., the annual performance review). Given that every single team—whether it was a branch-based team or a sales team—learned weekly customer satisfaction scores and sales information, it was very easy to see the difference in performance of those teams that executed the coaching mandate skillfully versus those who did not take it seriously.

The difference in those customer service scores and overall sales performance is the reason I'm writing this book.

I had not met a company before my Commonwealth Bank experience that had executed the coaching concepts so well. Indeed, my subsequent search for other great companies that coach well was extremely tough—the ones I found are included in this book. What you need to know is that *coaching is the least used leadership tool that managers have available to them.* I will highlight the evidence for this later in this chapter, and I will also highlight research to show that it really hasn't changed much in the last few decades.

In fact, very few organizations are coaching their employees at even the basic level. Even the performance review, which is as close to coaching as many organizations get, is disliked by virtually everyone. In fact, 24 percent of employees actually *fear* the annual review while only 25 percent of workers receive more than one performance review per year.[1]

It's time, then, to put all the pieces of the puzzle together to ensure that we not only *design* a strong coaching system, where we create favorable conditions for us to coach effectively, and craft a strong feedback culture, but that we also *execute* the right kind of coaching with employees so that coaching is always effective, and that the *measurable* impact of coaching is determined so it is allowed to become a sustainable part of the culture of the organization. These three themes (design, execute, measure) are the foundation of this book.

Random Story #1: Surviving Australia

You may have guessed from this chapter that I'm very proud of assisting the Commonwealth Bank in going from the worst in terms of customer satisfaction to the very best in Australia. However, I'm more proud of the fact that I survived Australia itself. There simply are so many ways to die.

Funnel-web spider:
almost as aggressive as Australians

Of course, you know the obvious ones, such as crocodiles, sharks, and snakes, but let me tell you, you haven't even started on the list of the terrible ways to die in OZ. Let's talk about spiders, and in particular, the Sydney Funnel-web spider. It lives in downtown Sydney, resides in swimming pools, and is absolutely unafraid of humans. In some bizarre twist of fate, cats and dogs are immune to the Sydney Funnel-web spider bite, but humans can die in 15 minutes from their bite. How did Mother Nature let that happen?

I could go on about the Blue-ringed octopus, that has venom 1,200 times more powerful than cyanide,[2] or the Box jellyfish, also having powerful venom, but the real menace is the kangaroo. One of the first newspaper articles that I read when I arrived in Sydney stated that 16 percent of all car accidents in Australia involve a kangaroo. Sixteen percent!!! Well, the first thing I wondered was, "so why do they let them drive? Take away their driving license and everything would be a lot better." But that's Australia for you. Think hard before you go.

More dangerous than baby-snatching dingoes

Increasing Employee and Customer Engagement

Let's play a game! Can you think of an activity that an organization can do to increase both employee and customer engagement simultaneously?

I win! It's coaching! When you coach effectively, not only are you increasing customer engagement because the employee will pass on more effective service to either an internal or external customer, but the employee's engagement also will increase as you are focused on increasing their capabilities, helping them make progress, and, most importantly, building their career.

Recently, with two co-authors,[3] I did a survey with 700 employees who worked in organizations across North America. We asked the employees where they worked, what kind of coaching they received, how engaged they were at work as an employee, and whether that coaching was part of a formal coaching program or an ad hoc program (if they received any coaching at all).

The results surprised us, but they are a fantastic reminder of the power of being coached by a supervisor/leader. Seventy-nine percent of employees in the survey who received moderate to high levels of coaching, based on 17 different dimensions of coaching,[4] said they were engaged at work. If they received low levels of coaching or no coaching at all, then only 46 percent were engaged at work.

Here is the twist: if the employees said they were part of a formal coaching program, but were not happy with it (i.e., the leaders said they were going to coach them and then they didn't turn up), then only 34 percent of them were engaged—the lowest engagement of all three groups.

The message here is clear: effective coaching drives employee engagement well beyond levels of those who are not receiving adequate levels of coaching. However, it is far better to do no coaching than to promise to do coaching and then not deliver on the promise. That certainly seems to be a recipe for low employee engagement.

Many other studies[5] have found strong evidence for a positive relationship between supervisory coaching and work engagement. These studies revealed that when supervisors/leaders engage in consistent coaching, there is increased engagement by employees because they have more energy, dedication, and absorption at work.

My favorite study (yes, I even like it more than my own research!) on the impact of coaching is by Latham, Ford, and Tzabbar.[6] This study looked, in particular, at the impact of coaching as it related to increased quality levels of the employee performance to deliver on the customer experience and also with the associated increase in customer numbers.

Their study investigated coaching using 1,500 mystery shoppers in three restaurants over 20 months. For 15 of these months, servers were coached based on the feedback they had personally received from these mystery shoppers (i.e., where the mystery shopper had identified what they had done well and what they can improve). Figure 1-1, below, shows the average server performance over time as coaching starts, gets reduced (the servers got less feedback in this period), and then finally stops in month 33.

The second diagram (figure 1-2) shows the impact of coaching on customer numbers in the three restaurants. The impact on customer numbers surges as the coaching is executed and then declines as coaching feedback is cutback and then stopped.

Figure 1-1: Server Performance Before, During, and After Coaching

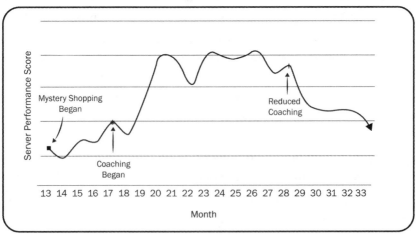

Figure 1-2: Customer Numbers Over Time

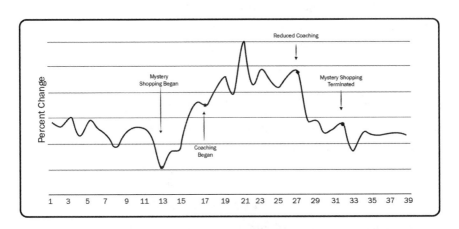

The two charts clearly reveal the impact of coaching in terms of increasing server performance and, subsequently, the number of customers coming into the restaurant. What is even more fascinating is what happens when the coaching finishes—employee levels of quality, while not returning to their original levels, are certainly lower than when the coaching was in full swing.

Many studies, in fact, show that when employees do get coaching, the impact is unexpectedly strong both financially and in terms of customer engagement. Other research has shown,[7] for example, that managerial coaching of employees has more impact on commitment to service quality than traditional managerial approaches, such as rewarding employees for service quality behaviors.

In the mystery shopping study highlighted earlier,[8] it was also found that for every one dollar of investment in a coaching program, the firm received a two-dollar return because of increases in employee service delivery behaviors and growth in customer numbers. Liu and Batt[9] also found significant performance benefits from coaching of employees and revealed that coaching of front-line workers in their study "translates into a monthly return of $18 over the cost of the $48 investment in coaching [per employee]."

In many ways, therefore, coaching serves triple duty. Firstly, you can engage employees. By actively coaching employees you are focusing on them and giving them attention. In particular, if you can link your coaching to their career development, as well as grow their capabilities in their current role through your coaching, then you will be engaging in one of the most important drivers of employee happiness.

Secondly, by coaching employees, they are better able to serve their customers regardless of whether they are internal or external clients, and this may have a positive financial pay-off.

Finally, each time a leader engages in a coaching session, he continues to develop his own critical leadership skills, as a leader not only is likely to learn from the employee he is coaching, but also gains the opportunity to reflect on his own leadership abilities.

Why Do I Need to Coach (or be Coached)?

Daniel Goleman (2000), in his famous article, "Leadership That Gets Results"[10] states: "There are six basic leadership styles. Each derives from different emotional intelligence competencies, works best in particular situations, and affects the organizational climate in different ways." These six styles are coercive, pacesetting, authoritative, affiliate, democratic, and coaching.

He further discovered that two of these leadership styles (coercive and pacesetting) have a negative impact on overall work climate while four styles are positive (authoritative, affiliate, democratic, and coaching). Obviously, we are interested in the coaching leadership style, so let's zero in on that.

In his research, he saw that coaching leaders helped,

. . .employees identify their unique strengths and weaknesses and tie them to their personal and career aspirations. They [coaching leaders] encourage employees to establish long-term development goals and help them conceptualize a plan for attaining them. They make agreements with their employees about their role and responsibilities in enacting development plans, and they give plentiful instruction and feedback. Coaching leaders excel at delegating; they give employees challenging assignments, even if that means the tasks won't be accomplished quickly. (Goleman, 2000)

A coaching leadership style is critical if you want your employees to reach their potential *and if you, as a leader, want to reach your potential.*

However, the coaching style of leadership is hard to find, as Goleman states:

> Of the six styles, our research found that the coaching style is used least often. Many leaders told us they don't have the time in this high-pressure economy for the slow and tedious work of teaching people and helping them grow. But after a first session, it takes little or no extra time. Leaders who ignore this style are passing up a powerful tool: its impact on climate and performance are markedly positive. (Goleman, 2000)

After observing leaders for 15 years, it has become clear to me that leaders aren't coaching because they don't see coaching as urgent—even though most leaders know it is important. They focus on the urgent items in their daily work even if many of these are not important (such as the occasional pointless meeting and the stream of insignificant emails) and subsequently don't dedicate time to grow their employees or grow the organization.

It's not that leaders couldn't make the time; they just chose to move coaching down on the list of priorities. My belief is that if organizations can get a significant increase in the number of leaders coaching their team (even if the team is just one direct report), then these organizations would get closer to fulfilling their role of assisting employees reach their potential while enabling the organization to be more successful as well.

Coaching could even provide physiological help, as research shows that[11] coaching others reverses the draining physical effects of *power stress* that so many leaders experience. It's long been recognized that stress can reduce cognitive capacities and decision-making. Indeed, the stress that leaders experience reduces their effectiveness and ability to think clearly. As Boyatzis (2006), the main author of this research, says, "We propose that leaders may better sustain themselves by balancing the potentially stressful effects of exercising leadership with the ameliorative effects of coaching the development of others." (p.17)

So, teaching leaders to formally coach others helps build sustainable leaders by reducing burnout and increasing performance. Perhaps much of this power comes down to our desire to make a difference in our organizations. Give people a chance to do this, and they are rewarded with a range of strong, positive physiological effects.

Can employees reach their potential without being effectively coached in the organizational context? The research shows, and I would agree, that it would be difficult.

Eric Schmidt, ex-CEO of Google and now Google Chairman, concurs. When asked for the best piece of advice he ever received as a CEO, his answer came fast and true: you have to have a coach.[12] Back in 2002, when a board member told Schmidt that he needed a coach, his (natural) reaction was, "Why do I need a coach? I don't need a coach. I'm an established CEO. Have I done something wrong?" After the board mandated that he find a coach, he learned how essential one had been to his career. He states, "Every famous athlete, every famous performer, has somebody who is a coach, somebody who can watch what you are doing, and say 'is that what you meant, did you really mean that thing?' and really give them perspective. The one thing people are never good at is seeing themselves as other people see them, and a coach really, really helps."[13]

Further recent evidence from Google suggests that being a coach[14] is the number one characteristic of an effective manager. As part of their research, they conducted double-blind, qualitative interviews with both high-scoring and low-scoring managers in terms of their effectiveness. They also collected and studied thousands of qualitative comments from employee surveys, performance reviews, and submissions for the company's Great Manager Award. (Each year, Google selects about 20 managers for this distinction, on the basis of employee nominations.)

Who Would Have Thought?

By examining data from employee surveys and performance reviews, Google's people analytics team identified eight key behaviors demonstrated by the company's most effective managers.

A good manager :

1. Is a good coach
2. Empowers the team and does not micromanage
3. Expresses interest in and concern for team members' success and proposal well-being
4. Is productive and result oriented
5. Is a good communicator—listens and shares information
6. Helps with career development
7. Has a clear vision and strategy for the team
8. Has key technical skils that help him or her advise the team

While in our hearts, we know this research from one of the best companies in the world to be absolutely true and no real surprise, Goleman (2000) notes that it's the least-used leadership style. Consider, then, the impact of this formidable approach to the success of an organization.

Case Study: The Power of Tight-Loose-Tight at Commonwealth Bank of Australia

I've mentioned Commonwealth Bank's use of sports coaching, which prompted me to write this book. Now it's time to outline how we executed this coaching framework inside Commonwealth Bank.

Most of my time at Commonwealth Bank was working inside the branches and call centers that were eager to perfect a coaching approach inside the organization. The idea was that we needed to be able to structure a coaching process that enabled us to execute the vision of being number one in customer satisfaction in Australia out of all five major banks (as I noted already at the beginning of this book, when I joined, they were last among the five major banks).

In my time at Commonwealth Bank, we felt that if we could further structure a coaching process that aligned to what we were trying to achieve from the customer service perspective, then we were more likely to be successful. Part of what was created was the "customer experience flow model" coaching framework, which revolved around the idea of sports coaching—observational-based coaching that inspired employees and guided them as to how they could improve in certain areas of the customer experience. In many ways this was like a *playbook*, a set of guidelines or *plays* to help the employee execute their experience perfectly.

During my time at Commonwealth Bank, the best leader/coach I met was Felicity Barrenger, Executive Manager in Tasmania. Her approach to using a coaching framework, continually innovating and being a leader/coach, is exemplary. Felicity's area of Commonwealth Bank has performed at a consistently exceptional level, compared in terms of coaching and customer service in the last 10 years, and is still a role model today. I talked to Felicity again to hear her thoughts on why coaching makes such a difference.

Felicity states that "coaching works in so many ways as it provides employees with technical skills, builds the relationship between employee and the team leader, and enables the coachee to be focused on her goals and the organization's goals at all times."

Felicity added, "[The customer experience] flow model which, if all steps are executed well, should result in 10/10 [customer experience rating]. It was first designed to help staff take control of the customer experience. We then built on it to include the key factors our customers were telling us we need to include for them to rate us 10/10. It certainly makes coaching easier, as we can establish where it is that staff member is going wrong with executing on the customer experience." She further noted, "From a coaching perspective, the fact it is scheduled for our staff ensures we are disciplined with this activity." As we will see in this book, coaching is all about creating disciplines.

The employees were motivated at the outset because they knew that coaching would happen, the coaching would be linked to the bank's vision of being the very best in customer service, connected to their personal goals, and the coaching was coupled with how team members were remunerated, and, finally, the coaching also was linked to the customer service surveys that were done every single week, in every single branch and call center where the questions in the survey were linked to the coaching framework. The employees couldn't help but be engaged.

Commonwealth Bank and Felicity demonstrate this better than anyone else by using what I call the *tight-loose-tight* approach, with coaching serving as the final *tight*. I always advocate for this approach in my workshops, as it is a simple way to think about employees' success. Consider this:

Tight: Make sure that all employees have set clear goals for themselves and have declared their career aspirations, that they are clear about the expectations leaders have for them, and understand the role that they play in helping the firm achieve its goals. This will mean that they start to feel a sense of accountability. Felicity was clear that their coaching system created this because the coaches were always turning up and coaching the employees, discussing their goals and using their coaching model to align expectations, and, importantly, ensuring all employees knew the vision of the bank through these continual conversations (which enabled them to see the bigger picture). As noted above, this first tight also relates to connecting employees' work with how they were rewarded (40 percent of their bonus was linked to customer satisfaction surveys, which is what they were coached).

Loose: Let the employees get on with it. Don't insist on doing it your way. (This requires quite a bit of bravery and trust on the part of the leader). As Felicity Barrenger said, "We want employees to bring out their personality with the customer, scripting takes it away. We give the employees a behavioral framework in which to operate and then empower them. I extend this to my managers as well; they know that I trust them, I set *very* clear expectations for them and then get out of their way. They have never let me down."

Tight: Inspect what you expect. Check-in with employees frequently; an important part of the final tight is follow-up with coaching/feedback to individual employees to help improve their performance and help them reach their goals. These, of course, are the coaching sessions themselves. By always turning up during individual coaching sessions and by using a coaching playbook (in this case, the customer experience flow model) to highlight where they can improve, then that final tight is created to help the employee understand if he is on the right track, and if he is performing at a higher level. This is done by then showing the employee the progress toward his goals.

Another interesting connection that Commonwealth Bank has with sports or an athletic approach to coaching is the use of the *physical* dimension of coaching. Great athletic coaches don't just help their athletes technically, but they also help them gain more energy (eat the right foods, hydrate, etc.). Felicity added, "Using the Health & Life Program across the business [Commonwealth Bank], we encourage Free Health Checks, opportunities to speak with Nutritionists, Massage Therapy, Fitbit competitions, personal trainers, and other ways to help employees have energy at work."

Overall, the example that Commonwealth Bank set with Felicity as the archetype is inspiring—it has a clear role for coaching, they link to the bank's strategic priorities, and they use the athletic approach to coaching ingeniously. It's an organization we can all learn from.

The General Absence of Coaching

Let's be clear that what is going on at Commonwealth Bank is rare. The Chartered Institute of Personnel and Development[15] interviewed 1,989 managers and employees to identify their opinions of and attitudes toward working life. Part of the study explored the range and execution of coaching activities by leaders. The results showed that nine out of 10 managers (91 percent, in fact) said that they sometimes/always coach the people they manage when they meet to discuss their workload, objectives, and any other work-related issues. Only 40 percent of their employees, however, reported this to be true. I don't want to overstate the case here as managers *always* felt they were doing more than the employees felt they were in every category of work life (e.g., giving praise and recognition), but nowhere on the survey was the discrepancy more pronounced than on the coaching dimension.

Clearly managers believe they are coaching when they are not. Further research[16] into coaching with managers and their direct reports also revealed that, in interviews with 438 employees and 67 supervisors, "Supervisors perceive that they are engaging in coaching behavior at higher levels than perceived by their employees." There could be many reasons for this leader-employee discrepancy, but it means that, if as a leader you are *coaching on the fly* or *coaching in the moment*, it's unlikely to be recognized or appreciated as coaching—unless this *ad hoc* feedback is linked to a more formal coaching program.

I don't want to kick leaders when they are down, but in a recent *Harvard Business Review* article, Scott Edinger made this observation:

> We hear constantly about the importance and value of coaching, especially in sales. But, the reality I have observed while working with hundreds of organizations is that a true culture of coaching rarely exists. In a survey I conducted a few years ago with a sales team in a Fortune 500 telecom company, I found an interesting contrast. Leaders reported that they spent a considerable amount of time coaching their direct reports and scored themselves high on their efforts—on average, just shy of the 80th percentile. Direct reports responded by saying that they'd received little to no coaching from their leaders and scored them low—on average around just the 38th percentile.[17]

Finally, only 17 percent of North American firms and 11 percent of international firms have long-term coaching programs.[18]

A major reason for the absence of coaching is very likely attributed to the fact that leaders are not being coached themselves. In her book, *Act Like a Leader, Think Like a Leader,*[19] Herminia Ibarra notes that in her research with 173 executives conducted in October 2013, only 10 percent of the participants answered "very true" when asked if a mentor or role-model inside the organization had helped them become a more effective leader. In her research, Ibarra discovered that the biggest sources of help to grow the leaders was external, in terms of training outside the organization (first), and support from friends and family (second). This is remarkable and, as Ibarra states, this puts "the managers squarely in a classic do-it-yourself transition."

Coaching, Mentoring, and Counseling

Another thing that could be holding coaching back is a lack of understanding of what a coach actually is, compared to mentoring and counseling. Here is how I differentiate the three:

- A coach works with the coachee's present reality and helps the individual to move into the future. Generally more structured in nature, these meetings are scheduled on a regular basis. Coaching is generally performed on the basis that the coach does not need to have direct experience of their client's formal work-related role, unless the coaching is specific and skills-focused

- A counselor helps resolve the employee's problems with the past so the individual can carry on more effectively with present day-to-day activities. If you are coaching someone who appears to be unable to resolve issues from the past, it is best to refer them to a counselor until they can focus moving from present to future goals.

- A mentor has already been through the issues the mentee is currently going through. A mentor uses his expertise and past experience to guide the mentee. This tends to be more informal and meetings can take place as and when the mentee needs some advice, guidance, or support.

The most important idea is that a coach works in the present; they're looking at the coachee's current competencies and they are working out a way, through coaching, to grow those competencies in ways which are meaningful both to the coachee and to the organization. A counselor generally focuses on the past to enable a person to cope with the present. Mentors, on the other hand, are critical to helping people have successful careers, but generally are not observational based and don't get involved in demonstrating behaviors they want the coachee to exhibit.

A coach is someone who consistently turns up to his pre-planned coaching sessions with the main goal of helping an employee grow. I do not believe a leader is a coach if he only coaches in the moment or if he only turns up once or twice a year to coach someone. You cannot be successful as a coach if you only turn up a few times each year.

How to Move Forward with Coaching

How can a good leader put his coaching wheels in motion? Plan to implement the following as soon as you arrive at work tomorrow:

- Make time for coaching. Recent research shows that the number one reason leaders don't coach is because they say they can't find the time.[20] Leaders must block the time off in their calendar and make coaching immovable. If you ask any writer, they will tell you that the number one success factor in writing is blocking the time off, writing in that block, and never moving it for anyone.[21] Coaching is no different. The second you put this book down, choose a worthy candidate and make an appointment for a coaching conversation in their schedule. NOW, thanks!

- Turn up frequently. At Commonwealth Bank, as I mentioned, our guide was to coach each employee 30 minutes every week. For many organizations this is not possible. However, only turning up a few times a year and pretending that it's coaching is unlikely to get you a great reputation as a coach. I would suggest that six to 12 times a year is the minimum amount of coaching sessions. That appointment you just booked for coaching that I requested above? Make it recurring.

- Move away from data-free coaching. We need to move away from coaching that is based on anecdotal feedback and the coachee's self-reflected observations (which are full of so many biases). Coaches have real credibility when the feedback is based on real data. Imagine coaching an athlete by asking them how you think they have played, or what you've heard about them from others. Make sure the coaching appointment you just booked is based on real data, such as observing a salesperson with a customer or an employee running a meeting.

- Be authentic. Wondering what this even means? It's one of the phrases people use such as "cheer up," thinking that the words themselves will make it so. (We all know that the words themselves likely could have the opposite effect!) But I have a deliberate reason for using it here. What I mean is act *like* a coach. Coaches *believe* in their coachees, they *inspire* them, they *connect* with them. The moment the coachee realizes the coaching session is all about him, and the coach also realizes it's about the coachee, well, that's a powerful moment indeed.

Me as a Coach!

I was startled to be asked, in a recent coaching workshop I was giving, how *I* was coaching my team as the Associate Dean at the Gustavson School of Business at the University of Victoria. I was not startled because I did not have an answer, but because I was surprised that someone would put me on the spot, in terms of asking me whether I was practicing what I was preaching. It was a business person from outside the University asking me—they clearly didn't realize that professors don't do that!

My answer to him, I'm glad to say, was, "Yes." Recently, I designed a structure where professors are encouraged to join, voluntarily, a coaching program within the Gustavson Business School.

Two professors are buddied up with each other, and they go into each other's classrooms twice a semester to observe each other so they can give feedback. We have both junior and senior professors sign up, and we mix people up as much as possible. In my coaching sessions, I have been surprised to find how much I have learned as the coach. By observing someone teach in the classroom, I've learned widely from the great teaching techniques I've seen and can later apply. In short, yes, I coach and, yes, I see the benefits of coaching every time we run the program each semester. And I know the students see the benefit, too.

I was also the coach of my daughter's soccer team when she was 11, but I was horrible at that, and I was not asked to return. Apparently shouting profanities from the sidelines is not great coaching in the sports context—who knew!?

Next Up

The rest of this book will delve into the seven other Moments of Power in Coaching. The next chapter is The Moment You Design a System for Coaching (so that coaching becomes part of the fabric of the organization). This chapter looks at the power of creating a system for coaching and integrating it across the organization.

Moment of Power 2:
The Moment You Design a System for Coaching

I love systems! Without systems everything falls apart. Yes, designing systems is hard, but I see this as a very good thing. If it were easy, there would be no way to use your coaching system and its subsequent execution, as a way to lead your organization to higher performance and drive your organization forward faster than others.

Having said that, roughly half-way through this chapter you will start to feel nauseous, but it's not the chicken you had earlier, it's the fact that you are feeling a little daunted by the task ahead of you. It's okay, I'm here to help. By the time you near the end of the chapter, you will feel better, especially after the American Family Insurance case, which shows us the way in terms of building a coaching system. Toward the end of Chapter 7, the nauseous feeling will have gone and will be replaced by positive expectation and excitement. Unless, of course, that chicken really was bad.

What you need to know is that there is so much power in creating a strong system for coaching, and then ensuring this coaching is integrated across the structure and strategy of the organization; the more coaching is integrated, the more likely it will become a sustainable part of the organization. It's the strength of the coaching system that will create long-term success with your coaching. Yes, you can make gains with an isolated coaching program, but these kinds of programs are vulnerable to sudden changes within the organization and ultimately tend to fade away. Building a coaching system must be our goal—even if the work is challenging.

I detail below, just for you, the elements required in an organization to support a coaching system. These include the importance of having a coaching strategy (a plan that identifies the priorities for coaching based on the needs of your employees, leaders, and the organization as a whole), the importance of measuring the effectiveness of coaching, and the importance of coaching education and development.

So, why exactly is the systems approach to coaching so important? Do we *really* need this approach to execute coaching? And do we have to do so across the whole organization? Excellent questions. I'm glad you asked. You can go straight to the top of the class.

Organizations as Systems

All organizations are purposeful systems (although some are more purposeful than others) consisting of several interconnected, interacting, and interdependent parts. Each part of the organizational system is called a sub-system—and the coaching approach an organization takes is one such sub-system. The idea is that each sub-system derives its strength by its association and interaction with other sub-systems. In this way, the coaching sub-system must be strong, too.

As a result, the collective contribution of the organization is greater than the aggregate of individual contributions of its sub-systems. Essentially this is about synergy and avoiding silos. The coaching practices that the organization undertakes should not be separated from what's going on inside the organization; the more the different elements of the system interact, the more effective the overall system.

A good example is coaching and organizational values. All the organizations that I have worked with have values that are advocated within the organization. However, many of these same organizations have not created ways in which employee behaviors are changed or reinforced to ensure these values are played out day-to-day.

Coaching can enable leaders to identify where and how employees can live the values of the organization. For example, if you were coaching an employee to run a more effective meeting, you would ensure that this coaching opportunity would link to the values of the organization. Let's assume an organization had the values, amongst others, of teamwork and creativity. When coaching, you would specifically highlight opportunities within the meetings where the coachee could encourage teamwork (by ensuring all participants in the meeting had a chance to talk) and creativity (by ensuring there were opportunities within the meeting for brainstorming new ideas), or reinforce the times when the coachee lived the values through their behavior in the meeting.

Clearly, coaching needs to link to the priorities of the organization as well as the department and team in which the coachee resides. If coaching is disconnected from the strategic direction of the organization, it is likely to be less successful, especially since the coachee is less likely to see how coaching enables them to be successful within the organization.

The Learning Organization and Coaching

MIT lecturer and author, Peter Senge,[22] is thought to be a leader on the subject of learning organizations. He describes learning organizations as places "where people continually expand their capacity to create the results they truly desire, where new and expansive patterns of thinking are nurtured, where collective aspiration is set free, and where people are continually learning how to learn together."[23]

In his book, *The Fifth Discipline*, Senge (2006) describes why organizations ultimately want to achieve "systems thinking." Systems thinking is the way to see the connections, links, or relationships between things. Instead of seeing parts and pieces of how things happen, it allows the interdependent whole to be seen. He identifies systems thinking as the "fifth discipline" because he believes that thinking systematically is the pivotal lever in the learning and change process. In this respect, systems thinking and the learning organization play two vital roles in this book:

1. We must ensure that we see coaching as part of a *system*, rather than a stand-alone activity. If we coach employees and we don't relate ongoing coaching to the parts of the organizational systems (e.g., strategic priorities, key processes, etc.) then coaching will never achieve anywhere near its potential.

2. Similarly, organizations must see coaching as an essential mechanism to help the organization learn. Coaching can assist employees to see the big picture and to distinguish patterns instead of conceptualizing change

as isolated events. In short, coaches foster practices that make systems thinking a normal approach to innovation and problem solving.

Apart from the fifth discipline of systems thinking, there are four other key disciplines that Senge outlines:

Personal Mastery—begins "by becoming committed to lifelong learning," and is the cornerstone of a learning organization. Personal mastery involves focusing on becoming the best person possible and striving for a sense of commitment and excitement in our careers to facilitate the realization of potential.[24] Coaching promotes the intrinsic and extrinsic benefits of personal mastery, recognizing areas of needed growth in the coachee, and being disciplined about those improvements.

Mental Models—"Our mental models determine not only how we make sense of the world, but how we take action."[25] Our mental models must be managed because they prevent new powerful insights and organizational practices from becoming implemented. The process begins with self-reflection; unearthing deeply held belief structures and generalizations, and understanding how they dramatically influence the way we operate in our own lives. Coaches bring to the surface then challenge mental models that hinder learning in the coachees. They can do this by sharing the actual data that supports (or doesn't) the many generalizations the coachee holds about the world. If their mental models are not based on real data, then those assumptions limit the coachee's ability to work effectively in the organization.

Building Shared Visions—Visions cannot be dictated because they always begin with the personal visions of individual employees who may not agree with the leader/coach's vision. What is needed is a genuine vision that provokes commitment in good times and bad and has the power to bind an organization together. As Senge (2006) contends, "Building shared vision fosters a commitment to the long term."[26] Coaches cultivate a shared vision among coachees through ongoing coaching and linking coaching activities to the direction of the organization and the goals and aspirations of the coachee.

Team Learning—Teams are important because organizations operate on the basis of cooperation, which means that organizations cannot learn if team members do not come together and learn in a supportive environment. It's a process of developing the ability to create desired results collectively and to have a goal in mind then work together to attain it.[27] Coaches create an atmosphere in which people feel safe to express their ideas and feedback across functions and levels and to harness the deeper synergy from team learning.

This team learning, and supportive context, is very close to the recent revolutionary discovery made by Google. *Psychological safety,* they found, was the key ingredient to make the perfect team. The project, known as Project Aristotle, took several years and included interviews with hundreds of employees and analysis of data about the people on more than 100 active teams at Google. Psychological safety is the "shared belief held by members of a team that the team is safe for interpersonal risk-taking and a sense of confidence that the team will not embarrass, reject, or punish someone for speaking up," and "it describes a team climate characterized by interpersonal trust and mutual respect in which people are comfortable being themselves." [28]

The crucial part here is that the *who* part of the equation didn't seem to matter—specific personality types, skills, or backgrounds of the team did not make any difference.[29] This is a great reminder that coaching can create this psychological safety and that we should not get fixated on *who* we coach, but *how* we coach. Great coaching, within a strong coaching system, can grow any employee and team, one in which all individuals are encouraged to bring their best and be themselves. We will see this theme emerge again in our next case, later in this chapter.

Clearly, coaching can be used to help any organization achieve systems thinking through the five disciplines that Peter Senge (2006) outlines. But, also it is important to remember organizations are systems and that coaching is a fundamental sub-system, so we must design a coaching system that is not only robust, but also integrates with the other sub-systems within the organization.

Now it's time to develop this coaching system, but first take a deep breath. It's time to put your feet up for another random story.

Random Story #2:
Using Your Accent to Get People to Listen

Being an Englishman, with an English accent, has enabled me to stand out a little bit in terms of getting people to adopt coaching. Everything in life is, at the end of the day, about influencing people, and if your accent helps to convince people to your way of thinking, well then, great (although, I have found that my accent doesn't seem to make a difference in England).

After living in Australia, China, New Zealand, and Canada, I have discovered that, generally, the London accent (some say I sound like Jamie Oliver) is well-received. To be honest, it doesn't work as well in Australia as there are a lot of English people and the Australians mostly hate the English (long story but revolves around The Ashes, Bodyline, "whinging Poms," and sending naughty convicts there). Whenever I teach something, outside of Australia and England, people seem to listen more carefully because of my accent, and this helps absorb the content a touch more. Brilliant!

However, it was when I became a football coach (soccer for those of you who can't speak properly) that the accent really became advantageous. In North America, it is generally presumed that anyone with an English accent is amazing at football. People make the natural assumption that my coaching will be to that same ability. But here's the rub: I'm totally awful at virtually every sport. In fact, my sports teacher at my grammar school in England said, "You are the most enthusiastic yet worst sportsman I have ever met." (These were his exact words!) He wondered how anyone so giftless could be so keen. As you can tell, this guy was a great motivator!

Because I have an English accent, though, when I coach (both football players and business people in my coaching workshops) participants follow my instructions carefully. Thinking of it now, I'd better turn this book into an audio book quickly. (I have the perfect face for an audio book, too.)

So whenever people ask me, "Mark, why do you still have an English accent even though you haven't lived in England for 25 years?"

I say, "Why would I give up the only attractive thing I have left?"

Elements of a Coaching System

There are three key parts to a coaching system. These are *the elements that need to be in place to create a strong system.*

Figure 2-1: Three Levels of the Coaching System

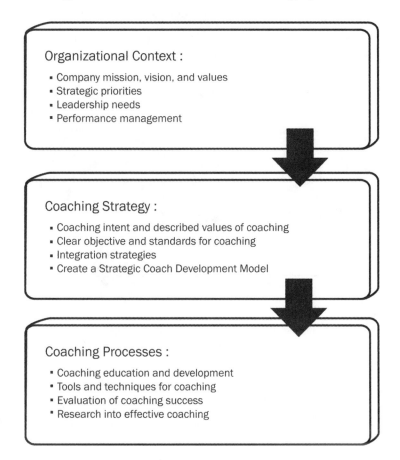

If the three parts of the coaching system connect, then you have begun to design a strong coaching system. First, the coaching strategy must be aligned to the context in which the organization is operating. For example, the coaching strategy should be linked with strategic priorities, performance management systems, and the values of the company. Similarly, the coaching processes, to execute coaching, must be clearly aligned to the coaching strategy. Education and training of the coaches must be related to the objectives and standards for coaching, for instance.

The more these three key elements are interrelated, the stronger the coaching system will be. Also, the system will be stronger, not only if these three parts are connected, but also if each of the three parts is individually robust. That is, if there are clear organizational strategic priorities, if there is a clear coaching strategy, and if the coaching processes are clearly developed, then the coaching system will be even stronger.

We now examine each part of the coaching system in turn.

Figure 2-2: The Organizational Context and the Coaching System

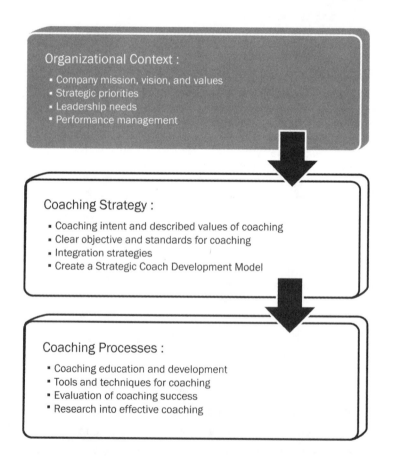

The highest level of the coaching system is an understanding of the organizational context within which coaching will operate and a coaching strategy that aligns to this context. The more the coaching ecosystem is related to what is going on inside the organization, the more successful the coaching system will be.

The idea is simple: The more coaching activities are related to the organization's current leadership philosophies, current values, strategic priorities, and performance management system then the more likely it is that the coaching within the organization will become sustainable, create measurable success, and be seen as logical from the employee's point of view. It's not that standalone coaching cannot be fruitful; it's just that it will simply make more progress if it is strategically connected with the direction of the organization.

At this stage of the coaching system, it is important to spend time with senior leaders in the organization to understand what their strategic priorities are, how coaching can help them achieve their strategic priorities, and in what ways coaching can be integrated into the organizational system to help the organization achieve its goals.

As we will see from the case studies later in his book, in particular the American Family Insurance and Joey Restaurant Group studies, at the end of the day, coaching is about helping the organization achieve its performance goals. The more time we spend understanding how coaching can assist the organization achieve its goals, the more successful it will be.

Coaching is a means to an end—higher performance of employees and the organization. In this context we must spend time understanding how coaching can drive the organization system forward and then bring this knowledge into our coaching strategy.

This is an ongoing process, as the organizational needs change constantly. We have to stay sharp to ensure that the coaching is always relevant and to understand whether or not it is making a difference.

The next stage of the coaching system is to design a coaching strategy that explicitly outlines how coaching will make a difference.

Figure 2-3: Coaching Strategy and the Coaching System

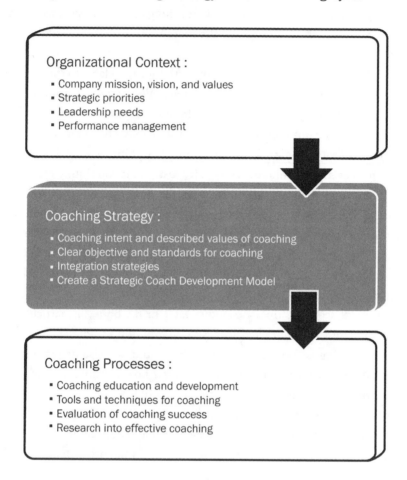

Organizational Context :
- Company mission, vision, and values
- Strategic priorities
- Leadership needs
- Performance management

Coaching Strategy :
- Coaching intent and described values of coaching
- Clear objective and standards for coaching
- Integration strategies
- Create a Strategic Coach Development Model

Coaching Processes :
- Coaching education and development
- Tools and techniques for coaching
- Evaluation of coaching success
- Research into effective coaching

If you want to make the best use of your resources and ensure that coaching has the greatest impact on your employees' performance levels, then a coaching strategy is critical to the organization.

A coaching strategy outlines your priorities for coaching based on the needs of your organization and the system as a whole. This allows you to set the direction of coaching and communicate your coaching intent and your described coaching values. This coaching strategy will guide the implementation of your coaching.

Organizations (or individual teams or working units, if that is the starting point for coaching) are encouraged to create a separate coaching strategy from the organizational strategy to ensure coaching gets the prominence it deserves. This coaching strategy should include the vision, and values, for coaching in your organization, team, or work unit. You should also include specific, measurable, and time-bound objectives for coaching.

The strategy should also include a strategic coaching development assessment—an assessment of current characteristics and size of your coach workforce. The core components of this assessment should be:

- Assessment of the current capabilities of the coaches—the current skills, knowledge, and behaviors of coaches compared to where the coaches need to be, based on the coaching strategy. In the American Family Insurance case study, later in this chapter, a redesign of its strategy meant that a coach's capability gap needed to be closed through training and education.

- An understanding of the stages of development of all coaches, at any given time, in their journey along a continuum from beginner to master. Again, the American Family Insurance case shows that measurement of the coaches' performance helps them identify areas they can grow.

- A coaching assessment—frequency, type, and quality of coaching currently occurring inside the organization.

- The availability of resources for coaching development. An understanding of the resources available means we will have realistic goals for our coaching.

This assessment is useful because it helps identify active coaches, the employees they are currently coaching, and the number and types of coaches who will be needed in the future. It helps to realistically assess what organizations can achieve in terms of coaching. It also ensures coaches have the appropriate skills, knowledge, and behavior to meet participant needs.

There also needs to be clear integration strategies in which leaders are proactively ensuring that coaching is connected to the overall organizational priorities. An example of this is when leaders inspect employee performance reviews to confirm that the employees are connected to the ongoing coaching they have received.

Another benefit of a definitive coaching strategy is that it provides a clear picture of where the organization wants to go with its coaching and communicates to the leaders and managers across the organization about how to get there.

The coaching strategy, likewise, focuses resources on the key priority areas that contribute to achieving overall organizational strategic objectives, and also helps leaders, managers, and coaches recognize a successful coaching system. This strategy will allow more effective use of resources and the development of a coaching system that delivers excellent coaching because the coach is better equipped to deliver a better experience for employees and their organization. The key is to involve leaders and managers to create a story that sells the shared vision of coaching, in simple terms, and to ensure organizational buy-in at every level.

Figure 2-4: The Coaching Process and the Coaching System

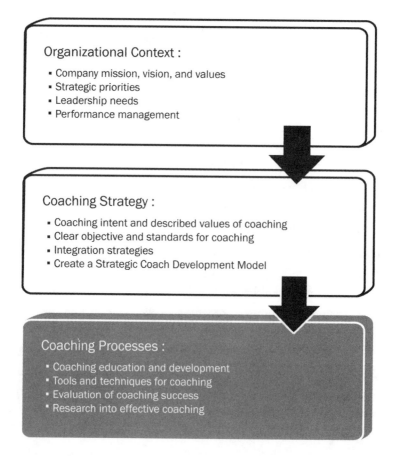

The final part of the coaching system is the on-going execution of the coaching strategy. The coaching strategy, described earlier, outlines described values, objectives, and standards for coaching. It also undertakes an assessment where coaching currently stands in the organization and outlines how coaching is connected to the organizational context. Once there is a clear strategy, then there must be a process for ensuring that there is a successful execution of the strategy. Consider the key parts to a successful coaching process:

Firstly, there must be an ongoing program for education and development of the coaches, so that they are continually raising their game in terms of the quality of their coaching and building their confidence in their abilities.

Secondly, we must ensure coaches have access to tools and techniques they can use to deploy successful coaching such as a coaching playbook (a set of usual tactics or methods that a coach can use to help the coachee grow in a particular area). At Commonwealth Bank we developed the Customer Experience Flow Model (see the case in Chapter 1), which was our main playbook to execute on an outstanding customer interaction.

Thirdly, there has to be a process for evaluating the success of coaching. The coach needs to understand that his coaching is making a difference, and that the goals that were set out in his coaching approach are being achieved.

Finally, there needs to be ongoing research into what makes for the most effective coaching. Continuous improvement in the quality of coaching inside the organization can only happen by looking for the best practices outside of the organization.

Let's briefly look at some of these parts.

Coaching Education and Development

Because organizations need skilled coaches at every level, the aim of educating the coach is to train and support their development, to meet the needs of employees, regardless of their pathways or environment.

In a recent survey of organizations that used either external coaches or internal coaches, it was determined that only 49 percent of those coaches were trained at all, and only 12 percent were in certified in any way.[30] Training and certification are important pieces, as we all have a strong capacity to be coaches, but, like learning to play an instrument, actual practice, study, and learning can make a significant difference. It is interesting to note that American Family Insurance (case in this chapter), Joey Restaurant Group (Chapter 3 case), and Delta Dental (case in Chapter 4) trained their coaches through formal external training.

Continuous professional development is crucial with varied informal and formal learning. Coaching education and development can take many forms (such as formal qualifications to simple sharing of internal best practices), but what follows are the most prevalent:

- A clear development program—a schedule for the different learning and assessment activities that a coach should undertake so they can become a better coach, usually over a 12-month cycle.

- An identified workforce of coaching educators—mentors, assessors, and strategists who can help coaches grow. These are the people who coach the coaches.

- Learning resources—teaching, learning, and assessment materials and calibration sessions available for the coaches (see Delta Dental in Chapter 4 as a great example of a firm who uses calibration sessions to drive learning).

- Quality assurance—systematic monitoring and evaluation of delivery of the quality of the coaching practices (see American Family case below as a great example of this).

Benefits of coach education and development are clear. More appropriately skilled and qualified coaches engage and retain more employees. Resources are used efficiently, utilizing the most effective way to support coaches to deliver at least to minimum standards of best practice. This leads to organizational coaches who are fit for purpose.

Tools and Techniques for Coaching

Successful coaching execution requires that coaches have access to tools and techniques to ensure they make an impact with their coaching. Coaches simply don't have the time to discover the best tools and techniques to do the best job. Finding such tools is the job of the *head coach*. For example, coaches need a playbook—plays that leaders and managers can coach toward that will enable them to improve the skills of the team. This could be a playbook on how to run a great meeting, or how to develop great customer service skills, or how to make a successful presentation.

There are hundreds of tools and techniques available for coaches today. The key is to let leaders and managers have easy access to these tools and techniques so they can get to the real job of coaching. Tools and techniques that slow them down or don't make sense to the coaches will only make coaching easier to resist and give them another reason not to do it.

Similarly, today's technology can make connecting with employees faster and easier than ever. Technology is a critical element to coaching, as teams are oftentimes dispersed around the globe, making ongoing face-to-face interactions impossible. Technology can help the coaches prepare for the coaching sessions, run the coaching sessions, and record the outcome of the coaching sessions. One of my favorites is CoachingCloud.® This cloud-based software provides an online platform to manage your organizational coaching. Coaches can connect online with the coachees through the cloud, allowing them to add value between sessions, which helps to develop a culture of coaching and a focus on improving performance.

The more technology can be used to simplify coaching, the more likely coaching will occur.

Measurement of Coaching Success

Another key part of coaching execution is the measurement that occurs to identify the impact of the coaching initiatives. It is critical to point to specific data about behavior change, as well as business impact through coaching.

Chapter 8 fully investigates how to measure the success of coaching. This practice is essential in building the case and confidence that coaching is making a difference. Suffice it to say that at this stage the evidence offered by the data that coaching is working means that the leaders who invest money in coaching are more likely to sustain their belief in the importance of coaching because they can see it actually makes a difference.

Five Levels of Coaching Sophistication

Based on systems thinking and the above coaching system, I have built a model that highlights the five levels of a strong coaching system. After working with many companies that have executed coaching, I realized that there are many different levels of sophistication of coaching. The goal of every organization should be to reach level five—the highest level of sophistication, at which coaching is used to improve organizational performance by showing employees how their work relates to and impacts other employees in the organization—this is systems thinking.

However, even achieving level one can provide many benefits for an organization. The idea is that by providing this framework you can diagnose where you are in terms of your coaching and subsequently identify the areas that you need to improve to move up through framework to level five. The idea of this framework is not to scare you, but to inspire you to achieve level five coaching, which is possible for everyone with careful planning and execution.

I start by outlining level one—building the base.

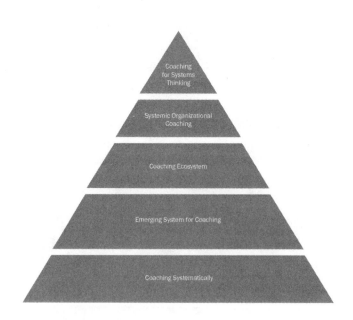

Figure 2-5: The Five Levels of a Coaching System

Level One: Coaching Systematically

The goal of level one is to deliver coaching systematically. At this level, coaches are authentic in their coaching activities and are consistent in their execution of these activities. That's it! Phew! Reaching level one is a huge success for any organization. When you are continually coaching your employees, then you are ahead of the game. Achieving level one, as Chapter 1 pointed out, is rare, so don't underestimate even achieving this.

Leaders who do turn up consistently to coach have conquered level one, but now need to turn to level two. Even though level one is a huge achievement, coaching is vulnerable in this condition, as it is not integrated into what the organization is doing as a whole. Measurement of coaching success does not occur and there is unlikely a systematic assessment and development of the coach's expertise.

Level two is where ongoing coaching is integrated into many other activities that occur in the workplace.

Level Two: An Emerging System for Coaching

Organizations at level two have established coaching structures that represent an emerging system for coaching by *implementing some vital parts of the coaching system,* such as creating a coaching strategy, clear objectives and standards for coaching, or the coaching is now linked to employees' goals and career aspirations.

However, at this stage some vital parts of the coaching system are still missing to prevent them from moving to level three—perhaps an evaluation of the success of coaching inside the organization does not occur, or maybe there is no ongoing education and development of coaches.

Critically at this stage, there is systematic coaching going on in most parts of the organization and there are some key coaching strategies and structures in place.

Level Three: Coaching Ecosystem

Within level three, organizations have developed a coaching ecosystem, which means that they have developed a coaching system that has *all of the essential elements of a successful coaching strategy and have executed this strategy.*

These elements include: a clear coaching strategy, established standards and values for coaching, links to employee goals, ongoing training and education of coaches, evaluation of the success of coaching, sharing of best practice in terms coaching with leaders who are currently coaching employees, ongoing assessment of capabilities of coaches, and the availability of sophisticated tools for the coaches so they can consistently execute high-quality coaching sessions.

Level Four: Systemic Organizational Coaching

At level four, there is systemic organizational coaching, which means that not only is there ongoing coaching inside the organization, but also a systems approach to coaching across the organization; the coaching program is *deliberately linked with organizational priorities and practices.*

Coaching supports what is going on across the organization, and there is a clear and continual overlap between the goals of coaching sessions and the goals of the organization. Further, there are integration strategies used to ensure coaching is connected with organizational practices, such as inspecting employee performance reviews to ensure they are connected to the ongoing coaching sessions.

Level Five: Coaching for Systems Thinking

At level five, not only are organizations systematically coaching and have developed a coaching system that is interdependent with the other key elements of the organizational system, but also that coaching is being used to promote systems thinking within the organization.

Systems thinking was described above—in the context of coaching, it means coaching the employee to appreciate how his work connects with other people's work. The more the employee realizes that his work can help or hinder other people in the organization, the more likely he will be to collaborate across the organization, leading the organization to higher performance.

All of the above sounds nice, right? But what does it all mean? The American Family Insurance case, below, shows us the way.

American Family Insurance: Building a Strong Coaching System

American Family sells auto, home, life, umbrella, business, and farm and ranch insurance. Located throughout 19 operating states, American Family's exclusive captive agents serve as local advisers to their customers.

I spoke with Tim Johnston and Eddie Dryer from American Family Insurance. Tim is the Director of the Sales and Service Care Center, and Eddie is the Sales and Service Care Center Administrator.

American Family Insurance is the best example that I have come across of a company that has created a complete coaching system. It even shows evidence of the highest level of sophistication with its coaching of level five behaviors—using coaching for systems thinking, which we will explore below.

In particular, what American Family does more than any other company that I have investigated is link its coaching to the organization's strategy, mission, vision, and values. As Tim says, "This is our North Star." Whenever the coaches coach, they ensure that the coachees understand the business context. For example, American Family Insurance's Mission is to "Inspire, Protect, and Restore Dreams" for its customers, and this is what the company aims for through the coaching process—to inspire its employees to protect their customers and meet their career aspirations and dreams.

This integration is critical—linking ongoing coaching with the direction of the organization seems to make an immense difference in terms of the credibility and sustainability of the coaching system.

The coaching program in the Sales & Service Care Center started a few years ago when the company's leaders realized that customer satisfaction scores were significantly higher for representatives who were licensed and able to provide many of the services an agent's office could provide. What they began to appreciate was that properly trained and professionally developed licensed representatives make a real difference. They also came up with a strategy goal of being the best in *operational excellence* in terms of the insurance industry in the U.S. But as Tim says, "This, however, meant significant changes in terms of how we approached employee development and our support model for agents and customers."

First, team managers were asked to spend a minimum of 50 percent of their time coaching people. This was a big change in terms of how they worked. Second, team managers had to come out of their offices and spend most of their time on the floor coaching agents one-on-one by listening to calls for in-the-moment coaching sessions. Previously, these structured one-on-ones were in the offices of the team managers, away from the actual work of the employees, which meant the coaching sessions were not based on live observational data, which has more credibility. Later in the book, we will talk about the importance of having real data when conducting coaching sessions.

Another key element of the coaching system was the Coaching Pulse Survey that they used (developed and administered by the Corporate Executive Board[32]). The survey enabled them to measure the success of their coaching (from coachee's perspective) and to see whether they were making improvements.

The Coaching Pulse Survey asks the coachees to critique the coaching they are receiving from the coaches. The latest survey conducted, in late 2015, reflected a statistically significant improvement from the previous year's results and demonstrated that the coaching was making a difference from the coachee's point of view. Customer satisfaction has also increased significantly, resulting in American Family upgrading its survey goal each consecutive year since 2014 from 9.11/10 in 2013 to 9.22/10.0 in 2014, and, subsequently, 9.36/10 in 2015.

Organizations with robust coaching systems measure the effectiveness of the coaching in as many ways as possible. In the Sales & Service Care Center at American Family Insurance, this further extends to the weekly *huddles* that they have, in which the team leader gets the team to huddle around a whiteboard then discuss their results—this is essentially a team coaching session around continuous improvement. This enables them to visualize success, which is a great way to show progress through the coaching.

The whiteboard approach looks at issues such as whether the team is hitting key performance indictors (KPIs), analysis of cost metrics and other performance metrics, like call-handling time and continuous improvement opportunities. As Tim says, "These huddles were awkward at first, as we adopted the coaching program with a more performance-orientated approach. But over time, they have become dynamic and vibrant, particularly as people see the results go up and they participate in the huddle conversations."

Another major part of American Family's coaching system has been its clear link to *lean methodology*. Lean methodology is about focusing on the value created for the customer and finding ways to continuously improve key processes. Coaching plays a key role in driving this mindset across the organization and sustaining it. Lean methodology has given the coaches a playbook from which to coach, and, as we'll see in Chapter 8, a huge part of the lean approach is coaching. Tim explains, "The lean methodology keeps things moving. It creates that consistency of approach, which you need when you are coaching on a continuous basis. Without the lean methodology, there is less structure in which to coach to."

Another key element of the coaching system, referred to above, is how it links the coaching to the employees' goals and career aspirations. It provides development opportunities within the department and also promotional opportunities to business divisions within the organization that need customer service acumen.

Another key part to this coaching system is formal training of the coaches and coaching evaluation. In terms of formal training, the team managers and other leaders went through the company's *Coach, Lead, and Succeed Program*. This formal training ensures that all the coaches have been through the same program, can speak the same language, and are more confident in their abilities because they've been through the same professional program.

Coaching reflection also occurs through the Coaching Pulse Survey. Based on the feedback from the coachees, coaches have to develop an action plan describing how they will improve their coaching. As coaching has improved, these action plans have evolved from being reactive to proactive. This means that, in the past, the area of improvement for the coaches was relatively clear based on gaps identified in the Coaching Pulse Survey. Now the coaches are encouraged to be more autonomous, in terms of how they feel they can grow as a coach, as opportunities identified in the Coaching Pulse Survey have become more limited.

Tim says, overall, coaching "has created a very transparent growth and development orientated culture, where people are not afraid to speak their minds and where there are open and honest discussions ongoing throughout American Family Insurance."

Eddie Dyer adds, "Through the constant dialogue of coaching, I think we have created a give-and-take culture that is based on collaboration. I think the consistency and transparency of the feedback is key."

In terms of level five behaviors—using coaching for systems thinking, Tim states, "This is present and part of our lean process—daily problem solving, Kaizen's, and Value Stream Connections. We also have specific questions pertaining to level five behaviors [such as sharing best practices with peers] in the Coaching Pulse Survey administered, and we score high in these areas."

Overall, this case is a great example of a systems approach to coaching. American Family Insurance has integrated the coaching system with its organizational priorities. It also has clearly created a strong coaching ecosystem (a clear coaching strategy, formal training and education of coaches, measurement of success of coaching, etc.) with demonstrable results. American Family Insurance represents a truly inspiring example of how to adopt coaching, execute it wisely, and achieve strong outcomes that can drive motivation and momentum for coaching.

Conclusion

Coaching is all about systems. The more that coaching takes a systems approach inside the organization, the more successful the organization will be. This means creating a coaching ecosystem so that the coaching program is effective. At a higher level this means connecting the coaching ecosystem with the organizational system so that they feed off of each other. And, at the highest level, this is about coaching being used to create a learning organization; one that is collaborative and in which coaching is used to teach employees that their actions are interrelated to everything else that's going on inside the organization.

The five-level framework of coaching is something for us all to aspire toward; the important lesson is to ensure that you are systematically moving from each level to the next level. Trying to run before you can walk, as pertaining to coaching, will only create more frustration. Get a program of coaching off the ground and then slowly build a system of coaching around it—one that includes a clear connection with the organizational system.

Moment of Power 3:
The Moment You Create the Right Context to Coach

In Chapters 1 and 2, we had the opportunity to set the foundations of coaching—understanding the power of coaching and appreciating the importance of building a system of coaching. Throughout Chapters 3-8, we will build on Chapter 2 to learn how to execute a coaching program—again noting that once you have created a system for coaching, then execution is much more likely to be successful.

For the next chapters, consider the diagram below:

Figure 3-1: Executing the Coaching System

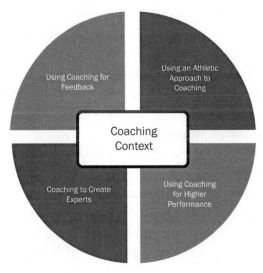

In this chapter we cover the context in which coaching occurs. It is based on the idea that what you do before coaching is as important as the coaching itself. Once you create the right conditions for coaching, then coaching is likely to be better received. One of the more powerful things you will read in this book is the notion that you can change the way people experience coaching by simply structuring and managing what they think or see before the coaching session itself.

What follows is a look at three particular conditions for managing the context of coaching.

First, we look at the psychological context in which employees are coached. The more we understand the psychological mindset of the coachee during a coaching session, the more likely the coaching is going to be successful.

Second, we look at the culture that is created inside the firm and the team—the stronger the culture inside the organization, as well as in the team where the coaching occurs, the more effective coaching will be.

Last, we look at the drivers of employee engagement. There is a significant body of research that pins down the key drivers of engagement at work. The more we understand each driver and the more we can link coaching to these drivers, the more effective coaching will be. I will provide examples as to how this can be done in a coaching context.

Power of the Context

Human behavior is sensitive and strongly influenced by its environment—in fact, more so than we ever realize. Social psychologists say that the golden rule of social psychology is that in a competition between the context in which you put an employee and their individual personality, it's the context that is most likely to drive their future behavior—not the employee's individual personality.[33]

For example, if you place someone who is fantastic at delivering customer service in a team that does not put the customer first and are more focused on themselves than being responsive to customers, then research indicates that the new employee will adapt his behavior to the team's behavior. He will slowly regress to the team's standards and deliver less than stellar service. Conversely, take someone who's never delivered a great day's service in his life and put him in a team that excels at looking after the customer. The employee will adapt his behavior to the team and eventually deliver world-class service, as the culture dictates.

Given the above golden rule, we need to think carefully about the context we create when we coach. The more we shape the context by understanding and shaping the firm's culture, the psychological context in which the employees work, and the key drivers of employee engagement, the more successful coaching will be.

Part 1: Managing the Psychological Context in Which Employees are Coached

The Chimp and the Human

Daniel Kahneman (2011), in his alarmingly good book, *Thinking, Fast and Slow*,[34] highlights the *dual-process* model of the brain. He reminds us that we comprehend the world in two radically opposed ways, employing two fundamentally different modes of thought: *System 1* and *System 2*. System 1 is fast; it's intuitive, associative, metaphorical, automatic, impressionistic, and it can't be switched off. Its operations involve no sense of intentional control, but it's the "secret author of many of the choices and judgments you make."[35]

System 2 is slow, deliberate, and effortful. Its operations require attention. System 2 takes over, rather unwillingly, when things get difficult. But System 2 is not in charge, System 1 is. System 2 is sluggish, and tires easily (a process called *ego depletion*)—so it usually accepts what System 1 tells it. It's often right to do so, because System 1 is, for the most part, pretty good at what it does; it's highly sensitive to subtle environmental cues, signs of danger, and so on. It does, however, pay a high price for speed. Kahneman (2011) notes that System 1 wildly jumps to conclusions, and is subject to a wide suite of irrational biases and interference effects (such as anchoring effects, confirmation bias, outcome bias, and the focusing illusion).[36]

Steve Peters (2012), in his book, *Chimp Paradox*,[37] gives another point of view in terms of System 1 and System 2. Peters calls System 1 the *Chimp* and outlines the science that demonstrates that the Chimp is five times more powerful than any other part of the brain (or, as Kahneman (2011) calls the *human* part of the brain, System 2). Because Peters is considered one of the world's leading psychologists and, among other credentials, has helped many an athlete achieve Olympic gold, we have every reason to believe that this is an effective way of looking at System 1 and System 2.[38]

Peters also introduces to us the *computer*, which starts life as an empty hard drive and collects our experiences, becoming a reference source for the chimp and the human to access. It stores values and beliefs, some of which can be positive and some of which are negative. Values are important, as they will be a guide to the chimp.

Figure 3-2: Chimp, Human, and the Computer in the Brain
—The Chimp Looks Like Fun, Until it Isn't!

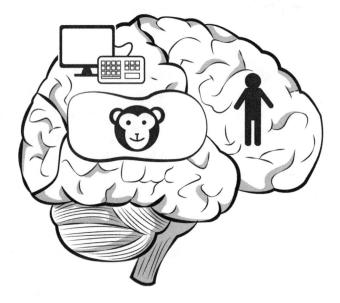

The point about the size of our misunderstanding of our own behavior, that Kahneman (2011) and Peters (2012) both make, extends beyond the details of Systems 1 and 2. Thousands of other experiments have been conducted, right across the broad base of human life, all to the same general effect—we don't know who we are or what we're like, we don't know what we're really doing, and we don't know why we're doing it. And this becomes the power of coaching—it helps us see what we can't see alone. It informs us of what we are missing, helps us work out how to improve, and moves us forward.

The secret to this is in the computer Peters (2012) introduced us to. If we remove the negative beliefs and values, and replace them with constructive beliefs and values, then the chimp accesses the new information when making decisions (when the human doesn't even get a look in).

The constructive beliefs could be the positive organizational values that are instilled and reinforced through coaching, the importance of grit and resilience when things go wrong (e.g., when the coachee doesn't achieve her stated goals), the coach highlighting the importance of working with other teams in the organization (when competition seems a more natural response), or the coach reminding the coachee that a team member's behavior could be explained by the situation they are in, rather than because of personality traits, abilities, or motives (as we tend to do).[39] When we supply the computer with these constructive beliefs through coaching, then when we are faced with these circumstances in the workplace, the chimp will use these beliefs rather than the *gremlins* that have crept in there over time.

Self-Serving Bias

The second psychological context of which we must be aware is self-serving bias. This is a cognitive bias that affects how people view situations and assign responsibility for the causes of events. The self-serving bias *is the trend that an individual will take credit for successes but blame external factors when things don't go according to plan.*[40] The self-serving bias is an approach to protect or enhance an individual's self-concept.[41]

I recently worked for two large organizations, and in both cases asked that employees complete surveys before we embarked on our work together. In one case, we asked employees how they viewed their own efficiency and their team's efficiency. The figure below shows their perception of the team's performance relative to their own. The figures represent the percentage of employees who felt that their efficiency or their team's efficiency was *good or excellent*. As you can see, there is a huge discrepancy (75 percent versus 49 percent) in the percentage of people who felt that their efficiency was competent, while their team's was less so!

Figure 3-3: We always think we're more efficient than everyone else

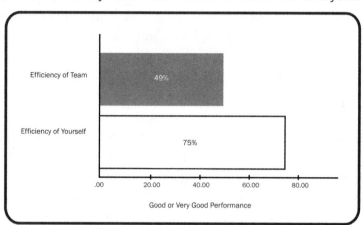

The second figure is from another survey in a separate organization and, in this case, the figure shows the respondents' answers to the question: "How often do you and your team display characteristics or take action in terms of taking ownership?" The figure shows that only around 107 respondents thought that the team took ownership *frequently or very frequently*, yet 156 respondents (46 percent more) thought that they took ownership *frequently or very frequently*. Both this figure and the above diagram highlight the power of self-serving bias.

Figure 3-4: We always think we own it more than everyone else

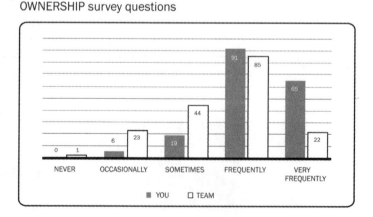

Self-serving bias, as you can see, is a common type of cognitive bias that has been extensively studied in social psychology and is probably one of the most powerful cognitive biases we have. Indeed, its effect on coaching is profound: If we think we are better than we are, then the practice of coaching will be less effective. If the coachee believes he is already proficient at what he does, then he will see coaching as fruitless or, worse, a waste of time.

It's critical that organizations ensure that coaches understand the importance of the presence of System 1 and System 2 and self-serving bias. If we understand this psychological context, it can make all the difference in helping the coachee recognize where he needs to grow and his natural response to feedback—whether it is good or bad. If we carry on coaching without recognizing the untrained chimp in us, and how our high opinion of ourselves might create a false reality of the situation we are in, then coaching will, clearly, not reach its potential in the organization.

Contrast Effect

If we see two things in sequence that are different from one another, we will tend to see the second one as more different from the first than it actually is. This is called *perceptual contrast*. Which leads me to another story…

Random Story #3:
Contrast Effect Used by Clever High School Seniors

So, everything in life is relative, right? You go on holiday to the same destination you went to the previous year, and you spend the whole vacation comparing that year to the preceding year, destroying the experience for yourself ("The soap was so much better in the hotel we stayed in last year"). Also, if you have more than one child, you will spend much time contrasting them ("Which of our children do you think is the worst behaved?"). My first introduction to the power of the *contrast effect* was in my last year of school.

When I was in my last year of school, I was extremely popular. If you met me now, you would probably find that surprising. But let me tell you a story that makes it less so. Most Friday and Saturday nights, my friends would invite me to join them at the local bar (in England, the drinking age is 18, which most kids are in their last year of school). I liked this. I felt popular and part of the cool group. I have fond memories of that time. However, a few years after high school, when we all got back together during the summer break from University, one of my friends asked me if I knew why I was so popular. "Because I was fun?" I replied.

"Well, a little of that," he said.

Starting to feel a little uncomfortable, I asked, "So a lot of what then?"

"Well, it was also the fact that you were a great wingman," my friend replied.

"What do you mean by that?" I inquired, starting to feel a little queasy now.

"Well, when we were down at the bar and a girl walked up to us, we made sure she saw you first. Then, when she looked at us, we looked *so much better* in comparison. We found we were a lot more successful in finding dates on the nights you were with us."

Well, at least it was better than sitting at home.

And the contrast effect is very useful to know from a coaching point of view (and if you're trying to get a date in high school).

One of the ways we can use the contrast effect in coaching is to juxtapose people's own abilities before coaching and after a series of coaching sessions. The power of progress was highlighted in some fantastic research by Teresa Amabile and Stephen Kramer in their book, *The Progress Principle: Using Small Wins to Ignite Joy, Engagement, and Creativity at Work.*[42] Figure 3-5 below shows that 76 percent of diarists, who kept a diary on their best and worst days at work, mentioned feeling progress on their best days—far higher than any other mentioned event (please also see the importance of collaboration on best and worst days—we will talk about collaboration in the next culture section).

Figure 3-5: The Progress Principle

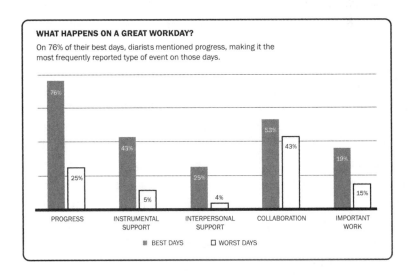

When employees feel like they are making progress in their technical abilities or they are making progress toward the goals set out in the coaching sessions, there is a great chance it will lead to one of their best days at work. It taps into the contrast effect—when we compare our abilities *now* to where they were *then*, we feel a sense of satisfaction when we see the difference and the advancements we have made.

It is essential that we try to provide contrast to coaches and coachees to highlight the difference that coaching is making in the organization, otherwise coaching simply won't get the shine it deserves.

Part 2: Managing the Culture in Which Employees are Coached

The second way that we can create the right context to coach is to create a strong and adaptable culture inside the organization where we are coaching. Strong cultures create a powerful context in which to coach, as employees are far more motivated to excel in a strong culture versus a weak culture. Likewise, having an adaptable culture means that employees do not rely on the past successes of the organization and become inwardly focused—they're always looking for ways to improve and grow. Research on strong cultures suggests that there are four dimensions to having a strong culture that will underpin successful coaching.

Alignment

The first dimension is alignment. Everyone is aligned to the same sense of purpose. When they understand the mission, vision, and goals of the organization and the team they are working in, *and* they are excited by that sense of purpose, then you have a key pillar of a strong culture. When everyone is pulling against each other, no one has a real, true sense of where their team, or the organization, is going. Obviously a lack of alignment also makes coaching much harder. When employees find it hard to make the connection between the coaching sessions and the direction of the organization, then the coaching sessions are less likely to be sustainable.

Conversely, if the coach successfully makes the connection between what they are doing in the coaching sessions and the direction and purpose of the organization or team, coachees are much more likely to make sense of the coaching.

This, of course, works both ways. First, the employee realizes his work can help the organization achieve its goals, and so he feels a strong sense of purpose, and also how the organizational goals are meaningful from the employee's perspective. When the employee understands and believes in the organizational goals, he is much more likely to work toward helping the organization achieve those goals. Essentially, this is level four behavior (see Chapter 2), where coaching is being used to connect what is happening at the organizational level to each and every coaching session.

This sense of alignment is also likely to lead to greater collaboration across teams, and this is where level five behaviors (systems thinking) can emerge. When the coach highlights how the coachee's role in the organization is connected to other people's roles in the organization and that he can help other people achieve their goals, as well as achieve his own goals, then the coach is really promoting the systems approach to running an organization through coaching.

A sense of alignment across the organization is a strong cultural trait, and a critical one, for a successful coaching system. The more people across the organization believe in the same things, drive toward the same goals, and are being coached toward achieving those goals in the context of their job, the more likely it is that the organization will get value out of its coaching.

Behavioral Framework

The second dimension of a strong culture is a behavioral framework. These are behaviors that are agreed upon across the organization as desirable behaviors for all employees. One of the more famous examples of an organization with a clear behavioral framework is Zappos.

Zappos Core Values:

Zappos employees live by 10 core values:

1. Deliver WOW Through Service

2. Embrace and Drive Change

3. Create Fun and a Little Weirdness

4. Be Adventurous, Creative, and Open-Minded

5. Pursue Growth and Learning

6. Build Open and Honest Relationships with Communication

7. Build a Positive Team and Family Spirit

8. Do More With Less

9. Be Passionate and Determined

10. Be Humble[43]

The key here is that these values are not only the behaviors that the Zappos team lives by, but also for which they have become famous. In most organizations there are certain values or behaviors that the organization's leaders have dreamed up, but in most organizations it's something employees only really see on an orientation day or hanging on the CEO's wall. But, as Tony Hsieh (2010), Zappos CEO, says, "What matters is that each of the core values becomes a natural part of an employee's everyday language and way of thinking. Committable core values that are truly integrated into a company's operations can align an entire organization and serve as a guide for employees to make their own decisions."[44]

The crucial insight here is that a behavioral framework drives strong company cultures, as it guides employee behavior and helps to ensure consistency across the organization. Without a strong behavioral framework, employees likely will lack a true sense of the behaviors they should display with each other and with the customer.

Hsieh (2010) goes on to say, "As it turns out, it doesn't matter what your company's core values are. What matters is that you have them and that you commit to them. What is important is the alignment that you get from them when they become the default way of thinking for the entire organization."[45]

While most behavioral frameworks occur through company values that are driven consistently throughout the organization, they don't necessarily have to emerge from the company itself. One of the key behaviors at Commonwealth Bank that changed everything in terms of excellence in delivering customer service was the core behavior of TOFU.

Not to be confused with rubbery food, the TOFU I am referring to is the acronym: **T**aking **O**wnership and **F**ollowing **U**p (the FU in most other organizations is something quite different). This mantra was not just for use with the customer but with each other as well, as we recognized that delivering service excellence to our peers was a prerequisite to delivering service excellence to the customer.

Again, the idea is that this behavior was driven by the organization through continual programs, communication, and feedback. In terms of programs, a few times throughout each year there would be *service and sales* meetings explicitly focused on TOFU, to ensure that everyone in the organization knew the importance of this behavior and discipline, and how to execute it on a daily basis.

In terms of communication, the CEO sent out an email every Friday with news of what had happened in the bank that week, as well as a customer service story about an employee who had exhibited a TOFU behavior—it was a great way to reinforce that behavior.

Finally, in terms of feedback, we did quarterly internal customer surveys, in which one of the questions asked was, "Did the internal customers who are serving you (e.g., Finance, Human Resources, Marketing) take ownership of your needs?" to track how well we were doing. To monitor the quality of the service we delivered to external customers, we also did an additional 3,000 surveys per week with customers who came into the branch or called the call center. Every single one of those surveys had a TOFU question on it so we could monitor progress of that behavior and provide feedback to each team.

The idea here is that the stronger and clearer your behavioral framework, the stronger your culture will be. Once you have a strong behavioral framework, you need to reinforce it at every opportunity to ensure the behavior is played out across the organization. Once this occurs, you have another powerful cultural trait.

In terms of coaching, having a strong behavioral framework makes it so much easier to coach because you know the collective set of behaviors that you are seeking to coach *across the organization*. This makes it easier to coach, gives you more content in terms of your coaching playbook, and, most importantly, enables you to reinforce these behaviors and allow them to flourish through coaching.

Communication

In the United States, there is a model that has been developed to encourage organizations to design themselves so they are most likely to succeed. These could be profit-oriented organizations, educational organizations, government organizations, or even sports organizations. The model is called the Baldridge Performance Excellence Program.

A few years ago, the researchers at Baldridge did an analysis of the areas that the best and worst performing companies (performance was in terms of how they scored on the Baldridge application) scored lowest on when applying for the Baldridge Award.[46] Amazingly, for both the best and the worst companies, the same phenomena emerged: communication. Yes, both the best and worst performing organizations had problems with communication—it is the one area of culture that organizations should never become complacent about.

To reinforce this point, consider another study including more than 1,400 leaders, managers, and executives about the critical skills and common mistakes made in leadership:[47]

Figure 3-6: Critical Leadership Skills

Most Critical Leadership Skills	
1. Communication / Listening	43%
2. Effective Management Skills	17%
3. Emotional Intelligence and Empathy	15%
4. Values and Integrity	8%
5. Vision	6%
6. Empowerment	6%

Communication was identified in the report as the most critical leadership skill. The study highlights that:

The ability to listen, read body language, ask questions, provide feedback, and generate effective two-way communication builds trust and can prevent performance problems down the road. In addition, the ability to comfortably use a variety of communication styles in order to articulate goals and objectives paves the way for healthy working relationships at every level within an organization. Providing relevant information allows employees to participate fully in their work.[48]

Strong cultures are built on strong communication whether this is through email, social media, town halls, or most importantly, face-to-face meetings.

To put it simply, you can't build trust through messengers. Communication needs to be open, honest, and two-way and can be both formal and informal. A key part of good communication is active listening. Strong cultures are built by leaders who know the pulse of the organization. While there are many modes for written communication, there is no substitute for face-to-face communication. It shows commitment to employees, and, through body language, builds (or breaks) trust. A leader who is accessible is respected, and one way to be accessible is to be a coach.

Similar to the other two cultural traits we have highlighted so far (alignment and a strong behavioral framework), communication and coaching are a two-way street. The stronger the communication from leaders inside the organization, the more successful coaching will be. An organization in which leadership continually communicates across the company, the more likely coaching will be conducted in the right context. For example, a key part of communication is transparency. When leaders are open and honest about what is happening in the organization, the more employees are engaged at work. Honesty is critical to building trust. Even when the news is bad, effective leaders tell the truth and don't shy away from communication. Employees who are committed to the organization will sense that you trust them and will want to contribute to solving a problem or help correct a difficult situation.

Along the same lines, coaching also can help with communication, as the coach can reinforce key messages that leaders need to send across the organization.

Collaboration

The final trait of strong cultures is collaboration. To have an effective organization, people must collaborate within teams and across teams. Silos simply cripple effective organizations. When teams compete with each other, withhold information from each other to create a position of power, or fail to understand the need to work together, the culture becomes grim. On the other hand, cultures that build in the need for collaboration and enforce the notion that people achieve more working together than working apart are great cultures to work in.[49] In the book, *The Progress Principle* (Amabile, T. and Kramer, S., 2011, see Figure 3-5), collaboration was noted as being the second event that occurred most frequently on an employee's best day at work. Profoundly, however, collaboration, or rather, the lack thereof, was the most prevailing event leading to an employee's *worst* day of work.

One reason that collaboration has become more important as a cultural trait is the increasing specialization of professions. As Morten Hansen (2009), the author of *Collaboration,* states, "The number of specialties in medical education that are approved by the American Medical Association has grown from 34 to 103 specialties from 1975 to 2000—that's a three-fold increase in just 25 years. Doctors, engineers, managers, designers, marketers, consultants, and also professors are all becoming more specialized."[50] This means that what Hansen (2009) calls *T-shaped management* has become more important. He explains, "T-shaped management is a simple idea: We need people who can perform their own individual work very well (the vertical part of the T) and also contribute effectively across the organization (the horizontal part of the T). They deliver two performances, not just one."[51]

Collaborative cultures are driven by three behaviors:[52]

- Disciplined collaboration: Collaboration is a means to an end, not the end. The end is better results. Collaboration is getting people to work together across departments, programs, or functions. Hansen (2009) notes, "Good collaboration amplifies strength, but poor collaboration is worse than no collaboration at all."

- Defining success in terms of goals that unite people rather than divide: this connects us back to the importance of the alignment cultural dimension.

66

- Adopting a collaborative leadership style: this creates ownership through leaders empowering their team to work with other teams.

In its simplest form, coaching is collaboration between the coach and an employee. In a coaching session, the two are creating a culture of partnership where there is recognition that employees helping other employees is an important and meaningful cultural trait of the organization. Likewise, when a leader coaches an employee, he is able to offer an opportunity to highlight the importance of collaboration within the team and with other teams in the organization. During their time together, the coach can identify how multiple teams can work together to achieve their goals through effective networking. They also can highlight the importance of getting the diversity of opinions in solving problems and identifying opportunities.

Ultimately, coaching is collaboration in action, but a collaborative culture created before the coaching begins helps immensely. Having this culture means the coachee understands the importance of partnerships and working together, rather than working alone, *before* coaching starts.

Table 3-1 below summarizes how each of the four cultural traits helps the practice of coaching and how coaching, in turn, can reinforce these cultural characteristics.

Table 3-1: Summarizing the Role of Culture and Coaching

Cultural Trait	How this cultural trait helps the practice of coaching	How coaching can help this cultural trait
Alignment	When employees are aligned to an organization's goals, he is more likely to see the importance of coaching—coaching helps move us forward toward these goals	Coaching can promote alignment because each coaching session can be connected to the employee's goals and the organization's goals
Behavioral framework	Without a behavioral framework, coaches often lack any playbook to coach from	Coaching can increase behaviors aligned to this framework because the collective set of behaviors that employees have agreed to is known, and can be coached to them in the actual coaching sessions (e.g., coaching to execute on an adopted organizational value)
Communication	Strong communication within the organization means the employee understands the importance of honesty and vulnerability within coaching sessions	Coaching enables clearer communication. The coach can communicate the goals of the organization, answer any questions the employee may have, and directly communicate how the employee can move forward through coaching. There is no easier way to have continual dialogue with an employee than through coaching

| Collaboration | When employees understand the importance of collaboration inside the organization, they understand the importance of collaborating with the coach because they understand more is achieved working together than working apart | Coaching, in and of itself, is collaboration in action. When a team leader coaches his employees, he is actively displaying that cultural trait. Similarly, coaching can help employees identify the importance of collaborating within their team and with other teams across the organization |

And now a case to show how culture and coaching come together!

Case Study: Joey Restaurant Group—
Using Coaching to Drive Culture

This case looks at Joey Restaurant Group and how they use coaching to drive their high-performance culture.

Vancouver-based JOEY is a group of 35 restaurants in North America, known for a globally inspired cuisine. It has nearly 4,000 employees, called partners, and an approach to staff relations more like a progressive corporation than a stereotypical restaurant.

It has been seven years since the Joey Restaurant Group embarked on instilling a coaching culture within its organization. Coaching is now an integrated part of the culture at all levels and is utilized by its leaders as one of many tools they have in their tool kit to effectively lead and manage.

As Andrew Martin, VP of HR, says, "We had a business purpose for bringing in coaching. Our growth was dependent on our ability to produce leaders. Leadership aligned on this point. We needed to develop 60 chefs and GMs over the next seven to eight years. This, from a current complement of 20! Coaching was seen as a way to expedite and enhance the development of our leaders, and this would support our business growth model. We didn't bring coaching in as a nice to do. It had a business purpose. If you are considering bringing in coaching, consider how doing this drives your organization's stated mission. If you cannot tie it back to this, you will likely have a tough time getting enduring support. We needed to accelerate the rate at which we could produce leaders. Coaching was a tool we felt could help us achieve this."

He further adds, "I kept open lines of communication with my bosses. I let them know what I was up to and why. I needed to ensure that they were fully engaged in what I was looking to take on. They were both outstanding through the process and that made the difference." Undoubtedly, senior leadership buy-in is critical to success. Without it, building momentum in a coaching program is so much harder to create.

Andrew then hand picked 12 people (affectionately called the "dirty dozen") to be the leaders in this endeavour. For this program to take hold across so many stores and across such a physical expanse, JOEY needed to generate a *fly wheel* of momentum through other powerful personalities. So they carefully selected regional representation, back of house, front of house, and head-office representation, and also chose those people who were influential and would inspire others.

They then took this group out of their jobs for three weeks over a four-month period. The purpose was to immerse them in coaching and also to get them prepared to teach aspects of the program to their colleagues and reports. During this process, Andrew was constantly taking temperature checks. Were people fully engaged? Did they believe in the program?

Joey Restaurant Group holds an annual leadership conference for which they fly out all of their leaders—now 170 of them. Andrew decided this would be an excellent opportunity to showcase what coaching was to the group. They had heard about it from the dirty dozen, so they had a bit of context. They decided that they needed to make this as impactful as possible, so they had the top coach in Canada (from Essential Impact, a third-party coaching company) coach their COO in front of these 170 managers (most under 30 years of age). It was high risk, but the coach and the coachee nailed it. At that moment everyone started to believe.

In terms of rolling the program company-wide, the first step was to deliver the program to all chefs and general managers. JOEY wanted them to get the training first so that they would be engaged in the program early, which hopefully would bring excitement to their teams. JOEY utilized the dirty-dozen influencers to teach portions of the program. This increased their engagement and again brought operational credibility to the program. If these 12 were behind it, then the participants would be behind it. The three-day course was a huge success.

"From there, rolling out the program was like pushing a rock downhill," Andrew stated. "It just rolled and rolled. I utilized the GMs and chefs to set the tone of the program, in much the same way that Al (the COO) had done at the conference. They showed openness and vulnerability to be coached on matters of importance. Opened the space for others to follow." They then created a coaching network as part of their coaching system, so that each person had a formal coach to work with.

Joey Restaurant Group has seen some great results, too. In 2011, they were awarded the International Prism Award for Coaching by the International Coaching Federation (they beat out the CIA and NASA). They also have been, for five straight years, voted as a top company to work for in Canada.

Anonymous internal surveys reveal coaching is being utilized regularly, and that it is having a positive impact.

Joey Restaurant Group has some advice for those who are thinking about including coaching in their culture. First, build momentum. Like most things, a coaching program needs to be fed. JOEY has created lots of momentum, but you still have to drive it. Also, remember there is a difference between coaching and giving advice, but there is time for both. You need to be clear on what the employee wants (advice or a coaching session) and what you are offering. There also should be a connection between coaching and performance. For this coaching program to grow and flourish, you must always connect it to performance and business objectives. Can you always answer the question, "How does coaching support your organization's mission?" Keep the link to the organizational purpose strong. As stated above, senior level engagement, in this case, the COO and the President, must always be evident.

Andrew summed it up by saying, "We have taken on coaching as a tool much as we use Microsoft Excel, or Microsoft Word, or a cell phone. We are not in the business of coaching. We are in the business of providing irresistible dining experiences. Coaching is in place to help us do this, and we need to keep the connection tight. We now want our leaders focusing coaching on how to help our people become more effective leaders. Other coaching will occur naturally and this is great. However, we need to ensure that coaching is driving our key objectives."

Part 3: Managing the Context by Understanding Employee Engagement

The final area where we need to manage context before delivering coaching is employee engagement. As noted in Chapter 1, coaching is the only strategy that companies can deploy that *simultaneously* increases customer engagement and employee engagement. You can increase customer engagement by raising the abilities and the motivation of employees to serve the customer through coaching; and when I say customer service, I do not differentiate between an internal customer and external customer. At the same time, you increase employee engagement because each time you successfully coach an employee, you engage them in their jobs, their sense of purpose in driving the organization forward toward this vision, and embrace the firm's strategic choices.

Fortunately, there is some very clear research on what the key drivers of employee engagement are. Once we know these drivers, we need to think carefully about how we tap into each of these drivers of employee engagement in the coaching session we're about to run.

This research on employee engagement is best summarized by Daniel Pink's book, *Drive*.[53] Pink (2011) summarizes his employee engagement research into three main drivers: purpose, autonomy, and mastery.

Purpose: People who find purpose in their work unlock the highest level of the motivation game. Pink says that it's connecting to a cause larger than yourself that drives the deepest motivation. Purpose is what gets you out of bed in the morning and into work a little bit quicker than those who don't have purpose. That also means that people who have purpose are motivated to pursue the most difficult problems. Elizabeth Moss Kanter, a professor at Harvard Business School, has formulated her own trio of motivating factors. One of the three is the same as purpose, *meaning,* she calls it. It is what helps people go the extra mile and stay engaged.[54] "People can be inspired to meet stretch goals and tackle impossible challenges," she writes, "if they care about the outcome."

Russell Benaroya, co-founder and CEO of EveryMove, a fitness rewards program, endorses this. "We are on a mission to give people a strong voice, to show that their healthy lifestyle matters," he explains. "Employees get up for that in the morning. They overcome obstacles for that. They care about something that is much bigger than themselves."[55] The benefit that the EveryMove

73

team experiences is the resilience to keep moving. "All companies face their own roller coaster of business ups and downs. What can employers do? Help employees connect to something larger than themselves. Get them out of mere measurement by numbers and figures, and connect work to people and values."[56]

Coaching creates purpose by linking coaching to the employee's aspirations and goals, as well to the organization's goals. The more alignment between the two, the higher their sense of purpose will be.

Autonomy: We're all built with inner drive. E.L. Deci and his colleague Richard Ryan[57] have explored the nature of what's called *self-determination theory*, a theory of motivation that takes into account people's psychological needs. They revealed, in a study of workers at an investment bank, that managers who offered *autonomy support* resulted in higher job satisfaction and better job performance. Autonomy support means helping employees make progress by giving meaningful feedback, a choice over how to do things, and encouragement. Workplaces can support autonomy by giving employees control over various aspects of their work—like deciding what to work on or when to do it. Virgin is one of the world leaders in terms of creating autonomy. As Richard Branson says, "We give our people real autonomy... We encourage employees to take advantage of flexible work hours: They can opt for alternative schedules, to work from home, or to work from one of our other offices."[58]

Coaching creates autonomy by putting accountability on the employee for their growth and by showing them what is possible. Also, by growing their skills, they then can undertake tasks and responsibilities that they could not do before.

Mastery: Mastery is the urge to get better and better at something that matters.[59] We want to get better at doing things. A sense of progress, not just in our work, but also in our capabilities, contributes to our inner drive.

Daniel Pink (2011) states that there are three parts to mastery. First, mastery is a mindset, in that we either believe we can get better or we don't (see Chapter 4 on fixed and growth mindsets). Second, mastery is painful, in that it involves not only working harder, but also working longer at the same thing. Finally, mastery is not a straight line, in that you may come close to, but never reach.[60] We will examine mastery in much more detail in Chapter 5.

Coaching obviously is all about creating mastery. By helping employees grow through coaching, in their respective domains, they are moving toward mastery.

Consider the following example as to how to use autonomy, mastery, and purpose in a coaching session, as well as a checklist for each coaching session, to ensure you have used these three drivers of employee engagement to the fullest.

Once you've read these two examples, please move onto Chapter 4—I have a surprise for you!

Example:
BUSINESS CASE

Coaching for Timeliness

Janet Wong opened her messenger program and pinged her colleague, Juan Gomez. "Running late. In a meeting. Start without me. I'll jump in as soon as I can," she wrote.

"Here we go again," Janet thought to herself. "I start early, and by 10 a.m. I am 20 minutes behind. How come this happens every day?" Janet scribbled a note: *Improve timing!!!!* Then went back to her call.

Later in the day, Janet went back to her scribbled note on timing. "The problem is back-to-back meetings," she thought. "No," she continued, "it is getting off the first call late, then having the second call go over. It's not just me, it is the calls, too."

Janet thought for a moment about what she could do. "The trouble is our culture. We do everything by conference call, and if one person is late, we wait for them. Then the call runs late. Things happen on the call, too. Some people want in-depth answers that the rest of us don't need. There has to be a way to take those discussions off-line and save us some time. Really, this is the conference call chair's role."

Janet thought about the chair for her first call that morning. Chen Day was a new employee and had a lot of technical expertise, but not a lot of experience managing colleagues. Being new, he was still feeling his way and figuring out how much he could ask of his team and his supervisor.

Janet thought about how she could use coaching to improve meeting performance.

Sample Action Plan Worksheet

Employee: Chen Day   **Coach:** Janet Wong
Problem: Recurring late meetings
Goal: On-time meetings
Timeline: November 2016-December 2016

Janet creates a set of actions to be taken through the coaching sessions and establishes clear measures of success, which are evaluated in subsequent coaching sessions. Examples below:

Action to be Taken	Measure of Success
1. Employee will manage calls so that calls start on time and end on time.	Tools, such as the Parking Lot and taking topics off-line, are used actively in meetings to ensure timing is managed. Clear agenda that is followed.
2. Employee controls talkative participants.	Employee seems confident in stopping others from trying to take over the meeting.
3. Manager/Coach will check in weekly (four meetings in a row) to inquire about progress.	Shows progress by highlighting data, coachee is happy with coaching shown through formal feedback.

Impact on AMP

Autonomy: If you are running effective coaching sessions on how to manage great meetings, then you are empowering Chen to properly execute the values of the organization and take control of meetings, even if they are challenging.

Mastery: Running a great meeting requires excellent organizational and people management skills. When you teach people to run great meetings, you're enhancing their ability to master an important task within the organization.

Purpose: If Chen will be more successful in his role by running the meeting himself, then we need to drive his sense of purpose forward by highlighting how running a great meeting will increase his personal brand and help him achieve the goals he set out through his coaching sessions.

Post-Coaching Session Checklist
(originally from Chapter 3)

After the coaching session, ask yourself:

Immediately
- Did I encourage self-direction? (Autonomy)
- Did I support skill development? (Technical or values based) (Mastery)
- Did I demonstrate how this staff person contributes to our vision or connect this coaching session to his career? (Purpose)

Continuously
- Check for progress
- Document progress
- Praise progress
- Continue to observe. It often can take months for a new behavior to become habit
- Listen for feedback. How is the employee coping with the change/project/growth? Can you help by removing obstacles, giving encouragement, enlisting additional assistance?
- Make modifications to the action plan, if necessary

Annual (Semi-Annual or Quarterly) Review
- Review goals and tie-in to firm's values
- Check for progress
- Review documentation—update as necessary
- Praise progress
- Share observations
- Collaborate to develop new goals—ensure tie-in to values/ strategies

Moment of Power 4:

The Moment You Realize the Power of Giving and Receiving High-Quality Feedback

To be honest, this book is not about coaching at all. I know this probably makes you very angry, as you have read the first three chapters already. Oh, so you only skimmed the chapters? Wait. You only skimmed Chapter 1? Wow, you need some coaching.

No, this book is not about coaching at all, and, yes, I should have said this earlier, but I was scared!

Actually this book is about feedback and growth; coaching is just a vehicle to provide feedback and help people grow. There are many ways to provide feedback, but frankly, coaching is the most useful, usable, and potent when it comes to giving *high-quality feedback* and helping people grow in the organizational context.

In fact, the whole notion of this book is that high-quality feedback is so critical, that it must be designed into the organizational system, so that it is methodical, authentic, and practical. But the only way to do this, I believe, is through coaching.

Most other ways of receiving feedback in organizations prove far weaker. Consider the usefulness of the feedback provided in performance reviews, for example. As noted in Chapter 1, for many organizations, these reviews are the only formal way to provide feedback—and it's loathed by virtually all.

Great employees demand great feedback. Brené Brown (2012) observed that a lack of meaningful feedback was the number one reason cited by talented people for leaving an organization.[61]

To consider the usefulness of any feedback that you have ever received, let's go back to school…

The Education System is Built on Low-Quality Feedback

Of course, this is a dramatic generalization, but let's be honest: The whole education system is built on summative (e.g., giving a grade) rather than formative feedback (e.g., useful advice on how to improve).

While it could be argued that many schools and education systems are different, when I look back at my own education, as well as on the many conversations I have had while reflecting on my children's education, any feedback received has been summative. Summative feedback with the absence of or limited formative feedback is what I call low-quality feedback. This is like the annual performance review, for example, that offers no or limited formative feedback. Even if feedback is given, the recipient is not really internalizing it, as it is mixed with judgment. This is also similar to an assignment handed back at university, which receives a grade and some feedback, but nothing prior to that—the feedback, at that stage, is mostly redundant, as the assignment is done, and the students have no opportunity to improve it.

Feedback, we know, is critical, especially in light of the research shared by John Hattie in his incredible book on learning systems called, *Visible Learning: A Synthesis of Over 800 Meta-Analyses Relating To Achievement.*[62] Hattie (2013) outlines those things that make the biggest difference in terms of student achievement; formative feedback (ongoing feedback rather than evaluative feedback), he notes, is **ranked third out of 138 influences on success**. Third. It trumps socioeconomic status, teacher-student relationships, problem-based teaching, parent involvement, and another 130 others! Formative feedback is critical for any achievement.

And, it's not just students and parents who thrive with this kind of feedback. Teachers, likewise, need and desire formative feedback. Bill Gates, in his work on improving feedback to teachers so they can be more effective in the classroom, discovered that 98 percent of teachers only get one word of feedback all year long, and that word is "satisfactory."[63]

Zero Sum Game

When I think back to my education at elementary school, high school, and university, I can recall zero feedback that I would consider to be useful. I often got summative feedback at the end of the assignments (and that varied in quality), but how much difference did it really make?

Of course, information from summative assessments can be used formatively when students use it to guide their efforts and activities in subsequent courses or assignments. But let's face it, the assigned work has been completed and, at that point, we are only using the feedback to justify our grade, and the feedback certainly won't help us improve that particular effort.

Annual performance reviews that most organizations undertake are almost identical—at that stage you are trying to understand how you got the evaluation that you received and whether it was fair or not. Are you are likely to reflect deeply on that feedback, or even listen to it as someone passes judgment on you? It's unlikely, isn't it? Even if you are not formally *judged* in that review, one annual formal assessment is unlikely to be useful feedback based on 1,600 hours of work.

I Don't Mind the Gap

A great example of a company that sees this issue clearly is the clothing retailer, Gap. Gap Inc. now does monthly coaching sessions between employees and management—known internally as GPS (Grow, Perform, Succeed)—instead of annual reviews. The idea is to focus on real-time formative feedback that helps empower employees to grow.[64]

The goal of formative feedback, as Gap has identified, is to monitor and improve employee growth to provide feedback, which can be used to improve his ongoing performance. More specifically, formative feedback helps employees identify their strengths and weaknesses and target areas that can be improved upon, and also helps coaches recognize where employees are struggling and address problems expeditiously.

This book is really about the benefits of using coaching to provide high-quality formative feedback.

The principle here is that clear, explanatory, and timely feedback to employees is essential for learning. Feedback that is occasional and cursory (e.g., saying "good job" or "satisfactory") is neither clear nor explanatory, and does not increase employee motivation or understanding. Clear learning goals help to increase the effectiveness of feedback to employees because the comments can be directly tied to their goals, and regular feedback prevents them from getting off track in their roles within the organization.

Relevance for Coaches

The feedback a coach offers can be most effective when it provides the coachee with specific information about a current state of knowledge and performance as it relates to specific goals. For example:

- Coaches could use formative feedback to relay to employees what they are observing and the strength of their performance by relating their progress toward specific goals.

- Coach feedback could incorporate information on what employees can do in the future to achieve those goals. For example, rather than general remarks, such as, "This does not appear to be working," coaches can make more directed comments, such as, "Your meetings are well organized and have excellent outcomes, but if you can get all participants to contribute during the meetings, then your goal of promoting collaboration in your team will be advanced."

- Coaches could provide feedback in a timely way (e.g., as quickly as possible after an observation of the employee) as this assists learning and is usually more effective than providing delayed feedback.

- Coaches could think about how the tone and targeting of feedback can affect employee motivation. We tend to respond better if feedback minimizes negativity and addresses significant aspects of work, in contrast to feedback that is negative in tone and focused excessively on details of performance that are less relevant to the learning goals.

- Coaches could think about feedback when employees are learning a new task or struggling with an existing one. Frequent praise following small degrees of improvement is very important, and when progress is evident, encouragement from the coach to persist can matter a great deal. Targeted feedback also can motivate coachees to continue to practice learning a new skill.

In short, coaching in organizations enables us to give high-quality formative feedback to employees more than any other vehicle that I know. As it is objective, based on data, linked to the goals you've laid out to the employee, ongoing, and each coaching session can build on the previous coaching session, so that it becomes more and more informative and helpful for the employee.

If you can think of another way of providing feedback that is more effective than coaching, I would love to hear about it. Please send me a postcard from where you live to Mark, Canada.

Three Paths to Using Feedback Expertly

To be a great coach and to be a great coachee requires a unique mindset and way of thinking. Organizations benefit when they educate their coaches and the employees being coached on the importance of the three paths that use feedback in the right way. Both the coach and the coachee benefit when all three paths are taken (rather than just one or two of them):

1. **Taking Responsibility for Feedback**—At the end of the day, organizations can coach all they want, but if the employee does not take responsibility for his own learning, the coaching will be a wasted resource. Douglas Stone and Sheila Heen[65] discovered in their research on how best to use feedback that, "The key player is not the giver, but the receiver."

2. **Demanding Feedback through Growth Mindset**—Employees and their coaches need to have a growth mindset—those people who have this mindset see effort, coaching, feedback, and learning goals as the path to mastery. The incredible work by Carol Dweck[66] on fixed and growth mindset shows that only employees and coaches with a growth mindset will be able to get the most out of coaching.

3. **Receiving Feedback Well**—The coachee must be able to use and receive feedback in the right way. If employees know how to receive feedback and how to use it to develop their skills, then coaching is much more likely to stick.

Let's look into each of these paths more deeply.

Path 1: Taking Responsibility for Feedback

In his book, *Compound Effect*,[67] Daniel Hardy talks about a seminar he went to when he was 18.

> I was invited to a seminar that I believe really flipped on the light switch of my potential. That day, those ideas changed my life forever. The seminar topic was *Responsibility and Accountability*, and we were discussing relationships in particular. The question was asked, "In a relationship, what is the percentage of shared responsibility in making the relationship work?"
>
> I was 18, so, of course, I had all the answers, and blurted out, "50/50!" The look on the instructor's face made it evident that my answer was incorrect. Someone else said 51/49, and explained you have to be willing to do just a little bit more than the other person. Someone else said 80/20.
>
> Finally, the instructor turned to the easel and wrote 100/0 and explained, "You have to be willing to give 100 percent with zero expectation of receiving anything in return. Only when you are willing to take 100 percent responsibility for making the relationship work, will it work."

In terms of coaching and using feedback, 100 percent of the responsibility is the coachee's. After all, they will lose out the most from not being coached effectively and not using the feedback to their advantage. The coach may not lose out at all. It is a magical moment when the employee feels accountable for taking the next steps, as determined from the coaching session.

But you can't tell employees that they are accountable for the outcomes of the coaching practices, you have to create that sense of responsibility so that they *own* the coaching outcomes. When the employee owns the coaching outcomes, the practice of coaching becomes a real way for an organization to grow.

This buy-in can be created through four ways:

1. At the outset of the coaching sessions, employees need to learn to recognize the importance of the coach's feedback and the difference that feedback can make to their growth and goal achievement. Remember, the employees are mainly interested in their own growth and in their own success (you must always remember self-serving bias from Chapter 3!), so if you can't demonstrate how the coaching sessions will make a difference to them and the organization, then the employees will never own the coaching practices. In these sessions it is important to clearly and explicitly define the coach and coachee's role and responsibilities. Finally, laying out the standards that will be upheld throughout the coaching process is key, meaning the coach must be specific regarding expected end results, time frames, and levels of effort.

2. Employees must be given a seat at the table. This means that the coach must ensure that the employee has brought his own goals into the coaching session and his identified areas for growth. If the employee feels like the coaching session is mandatory or imposed because they have no say in what that they are being coached on, or even how they are coached, they are, of course, much more likely to resist.

3. Employees should be held accountable to mastery goals rather than performance goals. Researchers have identified two broad types of goals: mastery goals and performance goals.[68] Mastery goals are oriented toward acquiring new skills or improving levels of competence. Employees who hold mastery goals are motivated to learn new skills or achieve mastery in a content area or on a task. In contrast, employees who adopt performance goals (e.g., where the main aim is to get a promotion) are motivated to demonstrate that they have adequate ability, or they avoid tasks in an effort to conceal a perception of having low ability. Performance goals can lead to the employee avoiding challenges if they are overly concerned about performing as well as their peers. In the typical workplace

situation, when employees encounter challenging situations, mastery goals are generally more useful than performance goals.

4. At the end of the day, seeing is believing. When employees see improvements and progress through their coaching, when employees see that the coach always turns up as she promised, when the employees see that the feedback they are receiving is high-quality because it is both usable and meaningful, then their sense of responsibility to engage in the coaching sessions will grow unchecked.

The simple idea here is that when employees are offered the opportunity for continual coaching, we must help them grasp this opportunity with both hands and help them become owners of the coaching process and their own continued growth.

Path 2: Demanding Feedback through Growth Mindset

If you push me hard, I would say Carol Dweck's[69] *Mindset: The New Psychology of Success* is probably the most important book on the importance of mindset written in the last 20 years. If you push me even harder, I will fall over onto my face. So, please don't.

Dweck's (2006) research focuses on why some people who are equally talented reach their potential while others simply don't. This is important research.

Dweck (2006) has discovered that people generally either hold a fixed mindset or a growth mindset. A fixed mindset holds the belief that traits such as intelligence and personality cannot be changed, and although people with a fixed mindset tend to believe that people still have the ability to learn new things, this does not impact their core intelligence or personality type.[70] Consequently, a person with a fixed mindset tends to process and understand a person's behavior or outcomes in terms of the person's fixed traits.

In contrast to a fixed mindset, people with a growth mindset believe that traits can be cultivated and changed, as people have the potential to become more intelligent through effort.[71] By conceiving personal attributes as dynamic, malleable qualities, Dweck and colleagues (1995) found that this may diminish the importance of traits in understanding behavior, while focusing more intently on specific factors such as needs and goals that support behavior and outcome (which is, of course, what coaching does).

To determine your mindset, consider how you view the impact of effort, challenges, and feedback:

Effort and Mindset

Probably the biggest difference between people with a fixed mindset or a growth mindset is how they see effort. Fixed mindset people see effort as a sign of low intelligence. Effort is for those who don't have the ability. As Dweck (2006) contends, "People with the fixed mindset tell us if you have to work at something you must not be good at it. People with a growth mindset believe something very different. For them, even geniuses have to work hard for their achievements. And what's so heroic, they would say, about having a gift? They [growth mindset people] may appreciate endowment, but they admire effort, for no matter what your abilities, effort is what ignites the ability and turns it into accomplishment."[72]

Dweck (2006) also says that another way of looking at it is that fixed mindset people see high effort as a big risk because if they try and fail, they are left without any excuses. However, growth mindset people see low effort as the big risk, as they see the notion of having a goal, but then doing nothing about it, as *the* big risk.[73]

We must also be careful not to see effort as the only part of achieving success. As Dweck (2015) notes, "Perhaps the most common misconception is simply equating the growth mindset with effort. We also need to remember that effort is a means to an end to the goal of learning and improving."[74]

Resilience and Mindset

Dweck and her colleagues (1995) also found a distinct difference in how people with a fixed mindset handle situations that result from setbacks, as opposed to those people with a growth mindset dealing with similar situations. People with fixed mindsets were found to be more likely, than people with a growth mindset, to react to a failure by questioning and doubting their ability. Furthermore, they were more likely to adopt a passive outlook in terms of successfully accomplishing similar tasks in the future.

Conversely, people with a growth mindset tended to focus more on behavioral factors in an attempt to identify reasons why they did not rise to the challenge. This led to the development of a new strategy that fosters behaviors aimed at improving their abilities as they continued to work toward mastery.[75]

In short, fixed mindset people lack resilience and grit and are more likely to give up in the face of setbacks. They also are more likely to avoid challenges, simply because they are afraid to fail. Growth mindset people, however, see failure as the path to mastery and because of this, they develop resilience and grit, learning to pick themselves up and face the next challenge.

Feedback and Mindset

The final area where mindset plays a major role is feedback. If you have a growth mindset you demand feedback so that you can grow and move forward on the road to mastery. Whereas fixed mindset people see feedback, particularly negative feedback, as something that defines them. They then likely will ignore, or at least discount, the feedback, given that they believe talent is the main driver of success, and not feedback.

In short, people with a growth mindset attend to feedback, and put it to work. One example of this is a neuroscience study conducted by a research scientist at Columbia University.[76] The authors of the study used a technology called "event-related potentials" to monitor students' brain activity while those students responded to factual questions and then received feedback on their answers. After the feedback session, the students were given an unexpected retest that included all of the questions they answered inaccurately the first time.

Students who held a growth mindset got more answers right on the surprise retest—suggesting they'd made better use of the feedback. Evidence from the brain-activation monitors showed something even more interesting, as related by cognitive psychologist Scott Barry Kaufman in his book, *Ungifted:*[77] "In terms of brain waves, participants with a fixed mindset showed an enhanced response in the frontal pole region to negative feedback about their ability. Because this area of the brain is associated with increased attention, it appears that the fixed theorists were more focused on what they got wrong than what they could do to improve. In contrast, the brain activity of those with a growth mindset suggested that they paid attention to the feedback and were more deeply engaged in processing that feedback." So, people with growth mindsets and people with fixed mindsets actually *process feedback information differently.*

Research suggests that a fixed mindset restricts the usefulness of feedback and will limit people's growth.

Summary of Fixed and Growth Mindset

A fantastic diagrammatic summary, by Nigel Holmes, of fixed versus growth mindset perceptions and outcomes is presented in the figure below.

Figure 4-1: Fixed versus Growth Mindset[78]

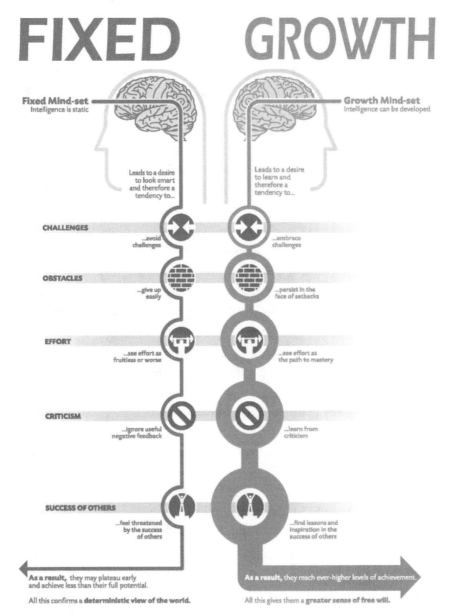

Delta Dental Case Study:
The Power of the Growth Mindset in Coaching

Delta Dental is a not-for-profit organization (with some for-profit affiliates as member companies). They have 39 independent member companies and offer national dental coverage—administering programs and reporting systems so they can provide groups and individuals with quality, cost-effective dental benefits. As America's largest dental benefits carrier, it covers more Americans than any other dental benefits provider, with the aim of making dental coverage more accessible and affordable to a wide variety of employers, groups, and individuals.

I spoke with Toni Roberts, vice president of customer service and operations, and Stephanie Rule, a supervisor fully dedicated to coaching at Delta Dental of Michigan, about its developing coaching system. Delta Dental is a fantastic example of how to build a sophisticated coaching system where the different pieces of the puzzle are connected and where there is clear evidence of the growth mindset at play. The company believes in growing people. It's as simple as that.

The new coaching system emerged as Toni Roberts realized that Delta's current approach to coaching was not working. Toni summarizes that "front line supervisors were responsible for coaching, but there were inconsistencies in their coaching approach; sometimes they got too busy to coach, and some simply did a better job than others. In short, supervisors were just getting through the day and squeezing in coaching where they could, and frequently the coaching would become negative as they were focusing on corrective behaviors, rather than the bigger picture of employee growth through honest feedback." Toni's new goal, therefore, was to develop a new approach to create consistency across the teams.

What they did was incredibly innovative in terms of designing this new coaching ecosystem. First of all, to create consistency, they turned two supervisory positions into full-time coaches. Their job was to coach—and nothing more. This created many benefits. First, they created consistency in terms of what coaching looked like. Each employee gets coached by one of the two coaches (roughly an hour every month). These coaches always turn up (because it is their only job), and since there is a coordinated approach between the coaches, this builds consistency and a strong relationship between the coach and the coachee. Second, the system is reinforced because the job of the frontline supervisor is to now take what the employee has been coached on once a month and have regular one-on-ones with the employee so that they can execute the outcome of the coaching sessions.

In this way, the frontline supervisor is still coaching (both full-time coaches and all front-line supervisors went through the same "coaching for success" training), but they are no longer the *head coach*. This removes some of the responsibility of being the only coach, which they found difficult to execute on, given all of their other responsibilities. Coaches and supervisors are regularly coached themselves so they can continually improve their coaching skills.

This is a great example of building an ecosystem where the head coach does the coaching and the supervisors help execute the outcomes of the coaching sessions. Another key element of the system at Delta Dental is to give the employees a seat at the table when they were designing the coaching tool (the quality control scorecard that is used to evaluate the coachee performance)— a true growth mindset approach. They did this by having two front-line employees on the committee, who designed the scorecard, representing the front line to ensure the scorecard was meaningful and appropriate to them. This meant they were much more likely to buy into the new coaching system as they had a voice.

Another major part of the system is the calibration sessions that they repeatedly have. These take two forms. The first calibration session is between trainers, supervisors, coaches, and Toni Roberts as the vice president. Toni recounts what happens: "We all meet together and listen to a variety of phone calls and each grade them individually on terms of the quality of those particular calls against the scorecard. We then come together as a group to discuss, and sometimes even argue over what were the correct standards are to have, based on listening to those phone calls. These calibration sessions are crucial, as they enable us to always stay on the same page and realign the system continuously."

Stephanie Rule, the supervisor acting as a full-time coach within Delta Dental adds, "We also calibrate by doing group coaching sessions with 10 to 12 people on the front-line. These are becoming even more powerful than individual coaching sessions as everyone gets to share their opinion and we all get a chance to agree on what is the right approach moving forward. Also, we build that sense of collaboration, which is crucial. We also make sure these groups are a mix of tenure, line of business, and age to ensure we get lots of diversity in these conversations."

Probably the most crucial part of the system is the fact that the coaching zeros in on the employee's sense of purpose by understanding his career aspirations and goals rather than "focusing on the numbers," as Toni says used to happen. When they started the new coaching program, they ensured that it was rooted in the employee's aspirations, which creates a growth mindset. Where did the employees want to go with their careers? How did they want to grow? How could the coach and the front line supervisor help them get there? The coaching is focused on better organizational results. That, of course, is the goal of any coaching program, but if you disconnect the coaching program from the employee's hopes and dreams, it is likely to struggle in the long-term. Any coaching program that simultaneously creates professional growth and personal growth is a great coaching program that locks into the growth mindset.

In fact, this approach has been so successful that the workforce, who happens to be unionized, told the human resources department "not to ever change the coaching program as employees love it and it really works for them." You know when the workforce gives you that kind of feedback, you are definitely on the right track!

Another key element of the system that Delta Dental has built is the tight-loose-tight framework introduced in Chapter 1; Delta Dental has executed it perfectly.

Tight—Make sure that all employees have set clear goals for themselves and have declared their career aspirations, that they are clear about expectations leaders have for them, and the role that they play in helping the firm achieve its goals—this will mean that they start to feel a sense of accountability. Toni was clear that Delta's coaching system creates this because the coaches are always turning up and coaching the employees, discussing their goals and using the quality scorecard to align expectations, using calibration sessions in a group context so that everyone is on the same page, and, finally, ensuring all employees know the vision and mission of the firm through these continual conversations which enables the employees to see the bigger picture.

Loose—Let the employees get on with it. Don't interfere with what they are doing or insist on doing it *your way*. (This requires a growth mindset, quite a bit of bravery and trust on the part of the leader). As Stephanie Rule says, "We are quite unique in that we don't have any scripting, instead we have a behavioral framework that we encourage employees to work within, and we make suggestions as to how they might be able to conduct a better call, but we definitely don't tell them how to talk to the customer. We create a sense of autonomy and encourage them to execute the call in a way that works for them, and this creates a further sense of accountability, too."

Tight—Inspect what you expect. Check-in with employees frequently; an important part of the final tight is follow-up with coaching and feedback to individual employees to help improve their performance and help them reach their goals. These, of course, are the coaching sessions themselves, which then also are reinforced by the frontline supervisor at Delta Dental. By always turning up once a month to have individual coaching sessions, as well as group coaching sessions, and by using a scorecard to highlight where the employees can improve, you then create that final tight to help them understand if they are on the right track. If they are performing at a higher level, show the employee the progress that they are making toward their goals.

Another critical part of having a growth mindset to coaching is that you are always focused on improving your approach. Delta Dental is dedicated to evolving its system to be more sophisticated. Two examples of this are: First, because the group coaching is becoming more important than the individual coaching, evolving the system to make more time for group coaching is something the company is working toward. Second, Delta is going to run boot camps, in which the focus will be coaching on a critical issue that everyone on the front-line needs to improve upon (maybe a new regulation change or new policy). These boot camps are exactly as they sound—short, sharp coaching sessions to improve everyone's performance in a particular area in a short space of time. This sounds a lot like Andrew Martin from Joey Restaurant Group, who stated that you always need to build momentum with your coaching program by feeding it and letting it grow. A growth mindset means that we never think our coaching program is good enough, and we are always looking for the next challenge in making it better.

The key result that has emerged, from Toni Roberts perspective, is the consistency of the customer experience through execution of the coaching scorecard. Prior to the coaching system being implemented, there was inconsistency in the quality of what the employees were doing. Now there is a higher level of consistency across the front-line. That is what coaching ecosystems create; consistency because of clear expectations, continual feedback, and, in this case, calibration sessions to ensure that everyone is approaching their work in the same way.

Overall, Delta Dental provides a fantastic example of having and building a strong growth mindset to coaching. First, by ensuring that all employees buy into the new coaching system by giving them a seat at the table. Second, by tapping into how employees want to grow, then using coaching to consistently give feedback to employees so they can actually grow. Finally, by growing the coaching system to continually make it more sophisticated. BOOM!

Personal Reflections on Growth Mindset

Ten years ago, when I first discovered Dweck's (2006) research on mindsets, I immediately introduced it into my work, both in my teaching and in my consulting. The impact it has had on people has been phenomenal.

Of course, many people in my classes or in the workplace have been raised with the growth mindset. Their parents taught them that effort, feedback, practice, and resilience are the keys to being successful. I find that while even people with the growth mindset reflect on how they could use this mindset even more to their advantage and how it has positively impacted them, it is instead those with a fixed mindset who use and are impacted by the mindset research the most.

I will never forget one encounter I had while presenting at a leadership forum for a large organization. Two female salespeople cornered me afterwards to say that they reflected on my presentation and that they both realized the effects that their fixed mindsets had about other successful sales people in the organization.

They shared that there were a couple of salespeople, in their internal team, who were very successful. The two found themselves talking behind the backs of their colleagues, often remarking how lucky they were for having a natural talent in selling. Their first thought, they said, was to put these people down and attribute their success to luck, better customer lists, etc. In reflection after my talk, however, sitting at the table and discussing it with each other, they thought that maybe they needed to rethink their approach, maybe these people just put in more effort, had been coached more successfully, and maybe were willing to do the things that they themselves weren't willing to do to be successful. The interesting part was that they were excited by this discovery, as if it opened up a whole new world to them.

Others have made similar comments, noting that changing their mindset had changed their life both professionally and personally. Similarly, I've even had many students tell me that they realize now that they've taken courses only because they know they can get top grades, and not because they might learn something. They further realize they should have been taking classes that challenged them, even if it meant lowering their GPA.

In reality, we all have a fixed mindset in many areas of our lives, as it is easier to believe that we either have the talent (I'm naturally good at this so

I don't have to work hard at it) or we don't have the talent (so why bother working) to succeed in particular areas. This makes life very easy in terms of the effort we have to put in and the feedback that we seek.

By believing that talent explains most of success, it makes it easy for us to focus on areas where we believe we are naturally good, as this does not require us to go through the process of practicing, acquiring a coach, and setting challenging goals.

The growth mindset can make a difference in all areas of life. For me, the growth mindset teachings have made an incredible impact on me as a parent. It is so easy to box your children into particular categories at being good at math or not naturally good at math, being innately creative or not, or having inherent artistic skills or not. It is also very natural for us as parents to praise our kids for being smart or intelligent, but as Dweck (2006) teaches us, praising kids for talent, intelligence, and achievement without the effort is the easiest way to give someone a fixed mindset because it downplays grit, feedback, and practice. The best thing we can teach our kids is that the success which is the most potent is the success we've achieved through choosing the right strategies, overcoming setbacks, and using feedback to make further progress in areas that we hadn't observed in ourselves.

Two words of warning: First, I am not suggesting that we have to put effort, practice, and coaching into every area. There are some areas in life we simply don't need to be great at, and that's okay. However, when we have a fixed mindset about the areas that might be holding us back, such as our ability to be a great presenter, or a belief that we can't be an inspiring leader, or that we lack creativity, then this is when a fixed mindset becomes problematic.

Second, don't use a fixed mindset to label people; this understandably has negative implications, and often this label will only make them angry and create more of a fixed mindset! The best approach to getting someone out of a fixed mindset is through continual conversations, showing him the progress he has made through the effort he has put in and, of course, coaching.

Now let's lose this sensibility and focus on silliness as we enter into very dangerous territory with Random Story #4.

Random Story #4:
Giving Feedback to Men versus Women

Yes, I am going write about the difference between giving feedback to men and women. This, of course, is where litigation starts, and my book sales tank. But let's be honest, men and women are different in how they seek feedback.

This is largely because men have only three emotions (happy, sad, and one more), while women have thousands of incredible, beautiful emotions.

One way, over time, that I've realized that men and women are different, is that women tell you pieces of information about themselves and then ask you to recount those pieces of information at a later date. For example, my wife recently asked me, "Mark, what is my favorite flower?"

I muttered to myself, "Darn it, I know this. I can remember this!" I breathed deeply and said, "Is it All Purpose flour?" Luckily, she thought I was joking and laughed.

Never has the difference between men and women become clearer to me than at Commonwealth Bank of Australia where we undertook an experiment across three different branches in Sydney.

We were experimenting on whether authentically complimenting a customer at the end of a nice conversation was a good way to add to the branch experience (we had a suspicion this would be true based on social psychology research). We had three endings: 1) no compliment, just the usual goodbye, 2) a loyalty compliment—"Thanks for your loyalty to Commonwealth Bank," 3) a personal compliment—"Thanks for being so lovely to serve, it's been a pleasure,"—this was the personal compliment that the tellers chose. Bizarrely, all the tellers in all of these three branches were female, so they felt this compliment could be used successfully with men and women.

We did this experiment with 495 customers (165 in each experiment). Endings were randomly selected. The personal compliment dramatically increased the number of 9/10s the customers gave the branch experience when interviewed by an external market research company as they left the branch. We realized then that complimenting the customer, genuinely, at the end of the experience made a huge difference to the perception of that transaction.

However, for every yin there is a yang. Unfortunately, what happened, in a few cases, was that when a female teller gave a male customer a compliment, he thought she was flirting with him and in turn wrote his phone number on a bank deposit slip and passed it through to the teller. We were astonished; the teller was only giving the male customer a pleasant compliment.

We now appreciated two things from this research. One, compliments are powerful—men in particular will believe anything women tell them. Two, we learned that men are sleazebags.

But then perhaps you knew that anyway.

Growth Mindset and Coaching

This research, obviously, has a profound impact on coaching, as employees with a fixed mindset are less likely to use the feedback from coaching effectively, less likely to take risks, less likely to rise to the challenges posed by the coaching sessions, and less likely to put in the effort from the commitments that arise from the coaching sessions.

Meanwhile, employees with a growth mindset will take on challenges posed through coaching and desire further coaching and feedback as they determine their own hopes for learning, rather than being focused on the outcome. It is in this context that employees learn to focus on mastery goals, rather than performance goals.

Obviously, this also has a profound impact on the coaches as well. If the coach has a fixed mindset about the people they are coaching then obviously this will play out in the coaching sessions, too. In many respects, it is far more dangerous to have a fixed mindset about the people you are coaching than about yourself.

Both the coach and the coachee, then, need to go through education sessions on the power of fixed and growth mindsets and the implications of each. Online there is a fixed and growth mindset quiz and a rating system, adapted from Dweck's (2006) work to enable readers of this book to assess their mindset, so they can gain an understanding of where they sit from a fixed and growth perspective.

Coaching With a Fixed Mindset

Much work by Peter Heslin, Don Vandewalle, and Gary Latham[79] (2006, 2012) has been done to examine the role that fixed mindset has on coaches. They have discovered that fixed mindsets impose an anchoring effect on initial judgments, regardless of whether they were formed directly or indirectly. Other work by Conger and Toegel[80] (2012) discovered that when a supervisor rates an employee for feedback purposes, his ratings tend to be based on judgment constructed as a result of information that was selectively noticed or remembered (i.e., they have a fixed mindset) about that particular person.

The results of these studies strengthen the confidence that the coach's mindset affects his recognition of improvements (or declines) in the performance of a coachee after an initial impression has been formed of an employee.[81]

Coaching With a Growth Mindset

Leaders must coach with an open mind. As Peter Heslin and Don Vande-Walle (2008) state, "Organizational effectiveness requires that personnel be managed, developed, and rewarded based on their actual performance, rather than managers' flawed perceptions of an employee's performance."[82]

The research of Peter Heslin and Don VandeWalle (2008) questioned whether a manager's mindset had an influence on the accuracy of performance appraisals and his engagement in employee coaching. The findings determined that the manager with a growth mindset was more likely to coach employees and integrate the coaching experience and outcomes with employee performance appraisals. In further research,[83] it was discovered that the degree to which managers have a growth mindset was positively linked to the awareness and ability to recognize improvement in employee performance compared to managers with a fixed mindset.

Further research by Heslin, Vandewalle, and Gary Latham[84] (2006) analyzed the importance of mindsets and coaching. They discovered that coaches who hold a growth mindset believe that personal attributes can be developed and that coaches are then, subsequently, more likely to make such investments in others. *Importantly, they also discovered that those coaches with a fixed mindset could be persuaded (through training) to adopt a growth mindset to increase the quality and quantity of their coaching.*

This discovery is critical because it means that even when a coach has a fixed mindset tendency about the people he is coaching, he can be educated out of that fixed mindset, so as to improve the efficiency and effectiveness of his coaching. And it reminds us that we cannot get a fixed mindset about those with a fixed mindset.

Path 3: Receiving Feedback Well

"I can't live, with or without you." U2

We need feedback to grow, but feedback is tough—hearing that we aren't perfect feels hurtful. And, even though we know the feedback will help us grow, the outcome is that serious effort will be required.

While it may be easier to live without feedback in the short-term, the results will be devastating in the long-term.

So, to begin down the path of understanding and embracing a growth mindset, the coachee must be able to use and receive feedback in the right way. If employees know how to receive feedback—how to use it to develop their skills—then coaching is much more likely to last.

Douglas Stone and Shelia Heen's (2014) book, *Thanks For The Feedback: The Science and Art of Receiving Feedback Well*,[85] provides further insight into how the receiver can best use feedback so that they can begin to learn and grow.

Clarify the Feedback

One of the best tips Stone and Heen (2014) give us is that we must first understand exactly what the feedback is telling us. It is often hard to know exactly what the coach is telling us, what exactly they saw, what they have recommended, and what we should do next. The critical point here is for the coachee to clarify exactly what the feedback is—restating your perception of the coach's feedback so that you are both clear on what the next steps are. Stone and Heen remind us that this clarification is particularly important when it comes to blindspots—when the coach says something that we don't believe is true or is unexpected. Clarification is critical.

Don't Shoot the Messenger

The second tip that Stone and Heen (2014) give us is that you must try to disentangle feedback from the person who is giving it.

It is important that the coachee listens to the feedback without trying to overlay any relationship tension that may exist between the coach and the coachee. Of course, we cannot ignore that relationship tension if it's going to get in the way of an effective coaching session, but we should at least do our best to separate the two.

Identity Crisis

Finally, Stone and Heen (2014) tell us that any feedback, unless it is only positive, is likely to impact our sense of identity. It may tell us something about ourselves that we do not believe to be true, or the feedback highlights an area we need to change that we find threatening. We may distort the feedback and magnify it in a way where the feedback becomes more important than reality actually dictates.

This may be particularly true at the beginning of coaching sessions when the coachee is particularly sensitive to any feedback he is receiving. This is where growth mindset training proves particularly useful as it allows the receiver to understand that the feedback can challenge him in ways that will help him grow and reach his learning goals.

In Conclusion: Building That Feedback Culture

Research has shown that a culture that intrinsically values and exemplifies a positive approach to feedback, perpetually creates growth opportunities in organizations.[86]

This research shows that employee development is highly influenced by leadership and the organizational climate that, in turn, contributes to feedback practices, interventions, and quality assurances within the organization.[87]

Organizations need to develop a culture where employees seek high-quality feedback. The more employees play a role in the feedback process and demand great feedback, the stronger the organizational culture will be. Coaches who do not turn up for coaching sessions, who are not authentic in their approach, and who do not put the employees first when it comes to coaching, should be rejected by organizations as cultural misfits.

This notion is central to this book: coaching will not happen without a strong feedback culture. Undertaking coaching because you believe that it is a good idea or that it is the flavor of the month is doomed to failure right from the outset. But the most important part of this feedback culture is that we hire employees and nurture employees to seek feedback and use feedback to move toward mastery in their chosen areas.

As we noted at the outset of this chapter, most organizations, both for profit or non-profit, do not give high-quality feedback to their employees. Nor do employees seek it. Coaching enables high-quality feedback to occur. In this respect, coaching is a means to an end. Just because we have a coaching system and great coaches does not mean feedback will be used or received in the right way—and this is vital to long-term coaching success.

The next chapter focuses on how we use feedback to move along the path of mastery, the next stage of our coaching journey.

Moment of Power 5:

The Moment You Use High-Quality Feedback to Create Experts

There is power when you create expertise in your employees. Coaching and feedback in organizations must have a purpose. What are you actually trying to achieve with your feedback? Coaching in organizations must focus on creating and growing expertise in each and every employee.

Remember Joey Restaurant Group from Chapter 3? You do? Brilliant! A weekend for two in Cuba awaits you as a prize! Just email me at cubascam@youhavebeenduped.com to claim.

Well, anyway, the company's feedback, through coaching, supports their main goal of creating a customized learning and development path for its employees called the "JOEY Path to Mastery." Through the JOEY Path to Mastery, leaders in the organization are given the opportunity to embark on different paths in their career in four distinct areas: business, leadership, coaching, and culinary. This *path to mastery* approach is one we should all take to heart—take a bow, Joey Restaurant Group!

The goal of coaching, therefore, is to create *masters* or *experts* by using feedback to help them on their journey and to integrate with other parts of the puzzle, such as external training and performance reviews.

In particular, we need to use the athletic approach to coaching to create experts in our organizations. The athletic approach to coaching is a multi-dimensional approach to coaching that successful professional athletic coaches use. This approach to coaching has been refined successfully for over a century and has much to offer organizations in terms of an established researched-based approach to coaching.

Throughout this chapter we will investigate why establishing mastery should be the coach's most important goal for employees and highlight where mastery comes from in music, sports, business, and, in fact, any area of life. We will then highlight the three key drivers in establishing expertise in any employee.

I then introduce the three dimensions of successful athletic coaching. These three dimensions have been developed over athletic coaching's 100-year history; and research indicates that there is a need for it to be adopted much more extensively in organizations. When employees master these skills, then you are creating expert employees who are more productive and engaged.

High-Performing Experts

A key proposition of this book is that coaching is a means to an end. In the last chapter we explored how coaching was a vehicle for high-quality feedback. But, where are we going with that feedback? What are we trying to achieve? Clearly, the feedback has to be directed into the areas that we have identified as important to the coachee and where development will help them.

Ultimately, feedback, through coaching, is the creation or development of high-performing experts. If employees are high performing, then not only will they reach their goals, but they also are helping the organization achieve its goals. But what does high performance mean? In the context of this book, we define high performance as *an employee who is continually growing his expertise and shows measurable results of this mastery* (see Chapter 8 on measuring coachee performance from coaching). An employee must move toward mastery and produce strong outcomes—without concrete results there is no evidence of progress.

Becoming an expert who can demonstrate clear outcomes is not an easy task, and coaching is essential to help employees achieve this.

The Irresistible Force of Expertise

Before we begin our journey on how to become an expert, let's examine why expertise is so important. From a customer's perspective, there is a moment during the interaction with an employee when she perceives whether or not she is dealing with an expert. This is an important moment in business. When an employee demonstrates that she is a reliable expert—because she is knowledgeable, professional, proactive, and has the customer's best interests at heart—this is a moment that cannot be trumped. The same is true for internal service when employees are serving each other.

Employees who show these qualities create trust and build credibility—attributes that are irreplaceable in organizations.

From a research perspective, the reliability of experts has long been shown to be the most important driver of service quality both internally[88] and externally.[89] Employees who keep promises, solve problems, and perform the service right the first time continuously have been identified as being employees who are demonstrating the most important driver of customer perceptions of service excellence.

However, the power of expertise runs much deeper than this. One of the main reasons we follow experts is because it makes life easier when it comes to tough choices. As Rhoads and Cialdini (2002) state,[90] "When feeling overwhelmed by a complicated and consequential choice, most individuals still want a fully considered, point-by-point analysis of it—an analysis they may not be able to achieve except, ironically enough, through a shortcut: reliance on an expert. It is for this reason that a communicator's expertise becomes increasingly important as issues become increasingly complex."

But it goes further still. As children, we are raised to follow people in positions of authority and follow their expertise—parents, teachers, and, in fact, anyone wearing a uniform (e.g., police officers and other members of the Village People) are constantly raised up as experts. This deferral is so powerful that it's been labeled a disease name—Captainitis.[91] This term emerged from incidents where investigators from the Federal Aviation Administration noted that, on many occasions, an obvious mistake made by a captain will not be rectified by the other crew members. Despite clear evidence of the captain's error, crew members give way to the *expert* and fail to attend or respond to a captain's, often fatal, mistake.[92]

To push this point even further, one of the best stories I've heard comes from Cialdini's (2009) book, *Influence*,[93] in which he cites the book, *Medication Errors: Causes and Prevention* (1981). One story is about the strange case of the "rectal earache." A doctor ordered ear drops to be administered to the right ear of a patient suffering from pain and infection. Instead of writing out completely the location "Right Ear" on the prescription, the doctor abbreviated it so that the instructions read, "Place in R ear." Upon receiving the prescription, the duty nurse promptly put the required number of ear drops into the patient's behind. As Cialdini points out, "Obviously, rectal treatment of an earache made no sense, but neither the patient nor the nurse questioned it. The important lesson of this story is that in many situations in which a legitimate authority has spoken, what would otherwise make sense is irrelevant. In these instances, we don't consider the situation as a whole but attend and respond to only one aspect of it." [94]

Obviously, this story is brilliant, but Yale University psychologist Stanley Milgram's[95] research on obedience to authority is equally brilliant. Milgram's (1963) experiments show how much we defer a sense of responsibility to experts or people in positions of authority, even when they may not actually be an expert. In one such experiment, the authority figure was an actor. Participants believed they were randomly chosen as the *teacher* and were asked to electrocute people when the *learner* (another actor) got a memory question incorrect.

Remarkably, two-thirds of participants electrocuted the learner to the point of death (or so they thought) when the learner no longer responded to the electric shocks toward the end of the experiment. Interestingly, the BBC remake, in 2009, found almost exactly the same findings as Milgram found in 1961. The results of the experiment were clear—when the authority figure told the teacher to carry on (after the teacher questioned if it was right to do so), the teacher almost always did.

While these examples clearly are negative, the idea is that when we meet someone who we believe is an expert, we will generally follow them—and that is a good thing as we must rely on experts to guide us and help us. The examples above simply demonstrate how powerful being an expert is—even if they have a dark side.

What Does Expertise Look Like from the Customer's Point of View?

Finally, before we learn how to create experts by using coaching, we need to look at the attributes of experts from a customer's point of view so as to coach toward those characteristics. During my time at Commonwealth Bank,

I coached hundreds of team leaders and employees working on the front-line, in both the call centers and in the branches.

After listening to and observing many employees, I discovered that there are two levels of expertise. Level one is *professionalism* where employees demonstrate expertise by being professional in everything they say and do. Level two is what I call *proactive expertise*. This is where I noticed that many employees move to another level by assisting customers in ways the customers didn't expect. Here, the employee passed off some of his power to the customer by educating them and putting them in control.

Level One: Professionalism

Level one expertise is driven by being reliable and by keeping your promises. This, of course, sounds completely obvious and you're now looking on Amazon to see how you get a refund for this book. But just think of all the times you've been let down by employees and organizations who simply haven't fulfilled promises made to you. How often have you been disappointed when an organization doesn't return a phone call or email when they have promised to do so? Organizations and employees simply drop the ball on this and need to be coached to ensure it stops happening.

Another very powerful part of expertise is the discipline we discussed earlier: TOFU (in Chapter 3). Customers love employees who take ownership (TO) and follow-up (FU) when necessary. Again, we need to coach our employees to take ownership of internal or external customers' issues.

Probably the most crucial part of expertise, and the one we can coach to the most, is knowledge. This is the technical part of expertise, and this relates to your expertise as a leader, as a salesperson, as a customer service representative, as an educator, as a negotiator, and the thousands of other jobs where technical skills and the knowledge that you gather from those technical skills enables you to fulfill the customer's request and answer their questions competently. Another big part of expertise is knowing where your knowledge stops, so that you can pass the customer off to someone with even more expertise. Coaching employees that they should fake their expertise is not a great long-term approach!

Crucially, another thing we must coach toward is the understanding of "The Curse of Knowledge."[96] The theory of the curse of knowledge shows why an individual, who knows something deeply, finds it hard to view a situation through the eyes of someone without this knowledge. It is difficult for them to relate to others who do not have their knowledge, *as they do not remember a time when they didn't know it themselves.* This is important because as someone grows their expertise through acquiring more knowledge, he often ends up talking down to the customer, using acronyms or language the customers simply do not understand. You can probably remember an experience when visiting a doctor who couldn't explain things in your language because of the curse of knowledge. Coaching enables the employee to understand when he needs take a step back from the knowledge and see it from the customer's point of view.

Level Two: Proactive Expertise

Level two expertise is where the employee passes off some of his expertise to the customer. Maybe the employee asks more questions about you or digs a little deeper to better understand your needs as a customer. This proactive questioning enables the employee to be more reliable when it comes to delivering on his promises.

Another major part of being proactive is explaining things carefully to the customer. Customers love being in control, even when they can't control the outcome. Whenever you take this approach, you are giving customers the gift of cognitive control.[97]

There are two kinds of control: behavioral control and cognitive control. Behavioral control is when you can give customers control over their choices or outcomes. For example, a financial planner who gives you a choice over the risk profile of the investments you could invest in.

However, in most cases we can't give customers behavioral control, but we can give them information, which makes them feel like they are in control. Cognitive control occurs when customers *feel* like they actually have some control over what is happening to them. For example, think of how you can track a courier package as it travels across the world. You have no actual control as to whether that package gets there safely and on time. However, you feel so much more in control if you can go online and find out where your package is at that moment and whether it will actually get to the destination on time. This gives you a feeling of confidence and comfort (but remember you do not have control over whether it gets there or not). And this is what great experts do and what you must do if you want to be perceived as an expert in your domain.

Overall, the goal of coaching is to create employees who are continually growing in their mastery through professionalism and proactive expertise. When the customer (whether they are an internal or external customer) walks away from an interaction with an employee, believing that employee has taken ownership of that interaction, has the right knowledge, has kept his promises, and has even managed to pass on some of his knowledge to the customer, then the customer is likely to believe the employee is demonstrating expertise.

The Making of an Expert

Happily, there is extensive research regarding how best to achieve outstanding performance through growing someone's expertise. K. Anders Ericsson is a Swedish psychologist and Professor of Psychology at Florida State University who is widely recognized as one of the world's leading theoretical and experimental researchers on expertise. Ericsson's research is so foundational that it has been used in many popular organizational books including, most notably, Malcolm Gladwell's (2008), *Outliers,*[98] in which he details Ericsson's work and uses his 10,000-hour rule in terms of the amount of time it takes to become an expert.

While Anders Ericsson has written hundreds of pieces on expertise, his most accessible research appeared in the *Harvard Business Review* (HBR) in 2007. In this piece, Anders Ericsson, Michael Prietula, and Edward Cokely[99] summarize expertise as being mostly explained by a combination of time, effort, deliberate practice, and coaching, where the coach guides the deliberate practice. It is my favorite HBR piece of all time, and I summarize it below.

Effort

The first step to becoming an expert is putting in the time and the effort to grow your expertise so you can produce measurable results that demonstrate that you are an outstanding performer. Ericsson, Prietula, and Cokely (2007) state, "Many people are naïve about how long it takes to become an expert."[100] Often, people believe that natural-born talent will enable them to become experts almost overnight. Ericsson, Prietula, and Cokely disagree. "When examining the developmental histories of experts, we unfailingly discover that they spent a lot of time in training and preparation."[101]

Just like the two female sales people in Chapter 4 and their perception that the most successful sales people in their organization simply had natural-born talent, we often attribute people's success in business, sports, and most other areas of life to innate talents, rather than the effort that must be put in. The research on expertise is clear though—without the effort, you will never be an expert.

Deliberate Practice

The second aspect of becoming an expert is what is called *deliberate practice*. Deliberate practice is practice "just outside of the employee's comfort zone."[102] The research shows that practicing within your comfort zone or only on areas you are already good at will not grow your skills.

Practicing too far out of your comfort zone means that you may continually fail and become disillusioned with the process, as you will not see any improvements. As an example, consider an employee who is trying to grow her presentation skills. If she is encouraged to make a major presentation in front of 80 executives from the organization early on in the process, there is a good probability that this experience may overwhelm her and hold the employee back from becoming a much better presenter. However, if she is asked to make a presentation in front of a small team of colleagues that she knows well and these colleagues are then asked to give feedback on that presentation, this is potentially a much safer environment in which to grow.

Probably the bigger danger, however, is simply practicing the things you are already good at, rather than the things you cannot do well presently. As Ericsson, Prietula, and Cokely (2007) note, "Research across domains shows that it is only by working at what you can't do that you turn into the expert you want to become."[103] It's natural for us to be coached on the areas that we're comfortable with already because succeeding in those areas is easy. Again, this is where having a coach is critical—discovering those areas where the employees can grow that are just outside of the comfort zone and then encouraging employees to deliberately practice in those areas.

The Role of Coach

The coach is the person who guides the effort, inspires that effort, and shows the coachee the effort that they have put in has paid off. As Ericsson, Prietula, and Cokely (2007) note, "The development of expertise requires coaches who are capable of giving constructive, even painful, feedback. Real experts are extremely motivated students who seek out such feedback. The best coaches also identify aspects of your performance that will need to be improved at your next level of skill."[104]

The coach enables the coachees to focus on their practice and provides the coachees with critical and timely feedback. This allows the coachees to engage in quality training exercises by selecting the right practice activities—the ones identified by the coach that stretch them beyond the current level of abilities.

Great stuff, right? Well, so is Random Story #5!

Random Story #5: How to Become a Shopping Expert

It's time for some coaching. In this instance, I will coach you to become a champion grocery shopper! If you get married and have kids, you may end up doing tasks and errands that you never really thought you would do, and possibly never wished to do. Many of these tasks make sense from the division of labor point of view—your partner takes on some tasks, and you take on others in order to divide and conquer. In my case, I became a grocery shopping expert simply because I had to, and now I would like to coach you on how to become an expert grocery shopper, too.

It all started when we got married. My wife initially thought she would do the grocery shopping. It turned out she generally went to the grocery store for about 60 minutes and came home with things like chipotle aioli mayonnaise, which we never use, nor have we considered eating. There would be a distinct absence of essentials, such as milk, vegetables, and other edible items.

I don't know if this was her particular strategy to get rid of the dull task of grocery shopping, but I took over, and, let's just say, because we have three kids, I spend a lot of time in the supermarket. Anyway, let me get to my point—I have developed an expertise that I would like to share.

Over time, I have realized that when I go into the grocery store, the best way to shop is to wander around for a few minutes to find someone who looks like me, and who has nearly finished his shopping (I don't mean actually looks like me because that would be weird, but I mean looks my age, and would likely have kids based on the products he has in his grocery cart). At some point in their shopping they tend to disappear down an aisle to collect something, while leaving their cart behind. At this stage I will pounce on the cart, dash off with it, and put one or two more items on top of said shopping cart, so the person doesn't realize I've taken the cart, and head straight to the checkout.

I urge you to adopt this approach to become a shopping expert as this strategy has a number of incredible advantages: 1) you get to complete your shopping very quickly, 2) you get to try new foods that you never would have thought of buying yourself, so the variety is amazing, 3) sometimes there is the added bonus of a wallet or purse left in the cart, which means you can make off with that too—although, in some countries, this is illegal. Okay, so sometimes you might end up with things in the cart that you don't need, like cat food, when you don't have any cats (you could always get a cat, I guess, to ensure the food is used), but the advantages sure outweigh the disadvantages, I find.

But What Type of Coaching?

We now have reached a crucial pivot point (and I don't mean because I've now taught you how to grocery shop effectively). Hopefully, this book has led you to a particular point where you understand that coaching is a valuable vehicle in which to provide consistently high-quality feedback.

Also, hopefully, you see the value of coaching and offering feedback to create experts in the organization who continually deliver the gold to their customers by being reliable, knowledgeable, and taking ownership. Finally, you also, hopefully, believe the research on expertise shows that there are no shortcuts to mastery—an employee must focus on deliberate practice, always continue with the effort (downplaying their natural talent), and demand high-quality coaching to ascertain the feedback that will enable them to put the effort and practice in the right areas.

If you agree with these principles so far, then I like you very much indeed, and I would like to have coffee with you (two espresso shots, please).

You undoubtedly have a few questions, like: How do we actually execute the practice of coaching, and what form does it need to take? Do I just turn up and coach? Do I give them feedback or are they supposed to work it out for themselves by me asking the right questions, rather than giving them advice? Does coaching mean I have to be observing them, or can I base it on other people's perceptions of their work? Do I have to do all the coaching, or can someone else coach them from time to time? Do I have to measure the success of my coaching or is the evidence for coaching so overwhelming that any coaching will make a positive difference? STOP! You talk too much! What do you mean Myers-Briggs says you are an introvert? Give me a break.

These are all fantastic questions, honestly, and you have clearly thought about this topic more carefully than I realized, but you need to let me carry on. After carefully examining many different models and frameworks of coaching and thinking about the best approach toward coaching, and after seeing its overwhelming success at Commonwealth Bank, I am convinced that the best approach is to adopt an athletic approach to organizational coaching. So, let me try to convince you that this is true as well.

Athletic Coaching

Athletic coaching and organizational coaching have close links for many reasons. First, Jerald Greenberg and Robert Baron[105] state that athletic coaches and organizational coaches share many commonalities of practice, including analyzing coachee performance, creating a supportive climate for development, and offering encouragement. Second, athletics and sports are a central part of our lives—many of us are first exposed to the notion of a coach through sports and athletics. Historically, the coach's role has been connected with sport as early as 1868, with coaching being associated with rowing at that time.[106] Third, this long, rich history of coaching in sports has led to research findings by Michael Read (2011) that suggests that organizations have not fully utilized athletic-based, high-performance coaching practices and that business can learn immensely from these activities.[107]

Though athletic coaching analogies are widespread within organizational coaching literature, omission of key athletic coaching practices in organizational coaching is likely to impact an employee's path to mastery. Bruce Peltier[108] (2001) suggests that a good deal of the athletic coaching literature aimed at business is based on clichés and simple motivational strategies. Lydia Ievleva and Peter Terry (2008) also report that even when sports coaches get involved in business, they tend to give motivational speeches to organizational audiences, rather than offering ongoing coaching or consulting. Consequently, the full application of athletic coaching practices to organizational coaching is an area of huge potential.[109]

Together with my colleagues, Read, Tax, and Corwin,[110] I outline the research that has examined different coaching practices that go on in organizations and in athletics, building on previous research.[111] Highlighted in our paper are 13 main coaching practice categories as shown in the table below.

Table 5-1: The 13 Main Coaching Practice Categories[112]

Coaching Category	Description of Practice Category	Usage by Coach Type
Bioenergetics	Coaches should know the nutritional needs of the coachee and provide information on nutrition and hydration.	Athletic
Coaching Effectiveness	Coaching creates better outcomes for the coachee, such as increased focus, motivation, better relationships, and collaborations. Attempts are made to measure these outcomes.	Both Athletic and Organizational
Demonstration	Coaches demonstrate their knowledge by acting out or simulating the desired skill. Leading by example and demonstration is as a good way for the coachee to model behavior after the coach.	Athletic
Confidentiality	Coaches maintain strict confidentiality during coaching and the delivery of feedback.	Organizational
Subject-matter Expertise	The coach has the ability and knowledge of the domain being coached to analyze individual technical weaknesses and prescribe practices to correct these areas of weakness.	Athletic
Feedback	Coach gives honest, specific, and positive feedback, which recognizes the coachee's characteristics that lead to a better outcome for the coachee.	Both Athletic and Organizational

Goal-setting	Coaches help coachees set effective goals and a plan of action to achieve these desired goals.	Both Athletic and Organizational
Handling Injury	The coach is concerned about coachee health and safety.	Athletic
Mental Training	The coach helps the coachee to prepare mentally and encourages the use of mental training tools to enhance learning and performance.	Athletic
Peripheral Resources	Coach helps the coachee by facilitating stakeholder cooperation, required resources, and coordination with other professionals.	Both Athletic and Organizational
Philosophy	A coaching philosophy represents a well-developed, predetermined set of guidelines a coach follows throughout a coaching program.	Both Athletic and Organizational
Physical Training	The application of exercise physiology is an important part of coaching. Coaches are advised to have knowledge of coachee physical training so as to optimize it.	Athletic
Practices	Practice may also be essential to coachee performance. In sport, planned practice is thought to be an important aspect of elite coaching. Consistent and prolonged practice is one strategy to improve coachee expertise.	Athletic

Overall, organizational coaches rarely utilized athletic coaching practices that dealt with *demonstration, subject-matter expertise, practice, mental training, physical training, bioenergetics (hydration and nutrition), and injury management*, while businesses tend to practice *confidentiality* more than athletic coaches, which is logical given the sensitive nature of topics being coached. The paper highlights the substantial opportunity for organizations to adopt a more athletic approach to coaching.

When I further reviewed the athletic coaching literature, it became clear that there are three dimensions of athletic coaching that we can use in the organizational context to further the practice of coaching.

These three dimensions came from an assortment of research papers on successful sports coaching; however, my two favorites come from researchers who asked world champion athletes how they were coached by their coaches. That is, what were the coaching techniques that the coaches used that enabled these athletes to become World Champions?

One piece of research by Natalie Durand-Bush and John Salmela (2002) explored four men and six women who had won at least two gold medals at separate Olympics and/or World Championships and were interviewed using an in-depth, open-ended, and semi-structured approach.[113] Another piece of research by Andrea Becker (2009) included interviews with 18 elite athletes (nine women and nine men) representing a variety of sports. These athletes, for example, had reached either the level of major league baseball, played in the NFL, were on the U.S. national soccer team or Olympic soccer team, or were players in a national basketball league.[114]

The research suggests there are three very different dimensions to coaching that coaches use to coach athletes who become high-performers.

The first dimension is *Technical Skills*. This is where the coach teaches the coachee to be skillful. Technical training is concerned with developing the required practical skills for the given sport or activity, and usually consists of predetermined drills while observed by a coach. Emphasis is on repeating patterns accurately for a sufficient number of times to convert a cognitive motor pattern (requiring coordinated concentration) into an autonomous one requiring little conscious effort. A major part of this is the quality of the technical training, as Durand-Bush and Salmela[115] (2002) share, "One element that stood out in the athletes' discussion of their practice activities was the quality with which they aimed to perform them. It was apparent that they focused not only on quantity but also quality."[116]

This was another strong theme within Andrea Becker's (2009) research. She states, "The athletes also spoke about the quality of their coaches' teaching methods. Specifically, they emphasized how their coaches paid 'great attention to the little details.' These coaches had the ability to 'pull out the finer things when teaching a player.'[117] And instructions were specific. They did not tell their players to 'just get it done.' Instead, they explained exactly how to get it done. The athletes also mentioned how their coaches simplified the process. One athlete explained how his coach 'always found a way to break things down to the most simplistic sense.'"[118]

These quotes reinforce the theme of Chapter 4—that coaching is entirely about high-quality feedback. When an athletic coach focuses in on high-quality feedback to develop an athlete's technical skills, they are creating **Mastery.**

The next theme is *Mental Skills*. Mental training focuses on how an athlete performs in mentally challenging situations and relates to an athlete's will and motivation to reach goals or objectives. In this situation the coaches narrow in on focus, the right mindset, imagery,[119] and self-talk, which is rarely used in the organizational setting. As Durand-Bush and Salmela (2002) state in their analysis of expert athletes, "Self-talk was a strategy that was utilized by all of the athletes…It helped them to remain confident, focused, motivated, and positive as they prepared for competitions."[120]

When an athletic coach focuses on an athlete's mental skills, they are creating **Focus.**

Finally, both of these pieces of research show that great coaches develop the *Physical Skills* of their athletes. This is different from technical skills, which are about creating mastery in how to actually execute their chosen sport. Physical skills are about athletes who are in their peak physical shape so they can perform at the highest level.[121]

This is achieved through appropriate management of stress, hydration, proper safety, suitable nutrition, and physical fitness. Physical training underpins both technical and mental performance by ensuring that an athlete can physically execute the technical movements and strategies at the required intensity and duration.

The physical component, the basis of any athlete's ability to play the game, includes all that is needed for a player to develop fitness and health and to prevent injury. When an athletic coach focuses on an athlete's physical skills, they are creating **Energy.**

When you put together Focus, Energy, and Mastery, you create experts as represented in the diagram below.

Figure 5-1: Technical, Mental, and Physical Skills to Create Expertise

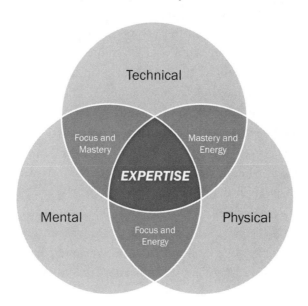

Now that we have established the case for adopting an athletic approach to coaching in organizations, we will now explore how best to execute these in the context of organizational coaching.

For example, how do you use coaching to create technical skills in organizations? What are the techniques for creating strong mental skills in employees in organizations? And what is the appropriate way to develop physical skills in employees in organizations given employees are not meant to be athletes? These are the questions we will answer in Chapter 6.

In the meantime, let's review a case study of an athletic organization I've worked with that has successfully implemented an athletic approach to coaching inside the organization—how ironic is that?

Case Study—Vikes Athletics

I've been working with the University of Victoria Athletics and Recreation department (codename Vikes) for three years now. Given that this is athletics and recreation, I first thought that it would be quite an easy task to introduce athletic coaching into running this organization. In fact, I likewise believed that bringing in coaching to enable the employees to raise their game in terms of providing better service, become better leaders, and be more productive in their work, would be relatively intuitive.

This, however, proved not to be the case. In fact, because athletic coaching was so ingrained in what they already did, they found it harder to make the leap into using this approach inside the organization.

Along the way we realized that we had to build a system around coaching so that coaching made more sense in the organizational context.

We created *The Vikes Edge* document, as shown below, to enable employees to understand how coaching fits into innovation, continuous improvement, and teamwork.

VISION

Together we transform students' lives.

PURPOSE

Excellence distinguishes us in sport & active healthy living.

OUR PROMISE

We foster an environment where diversity is valued, quality of life is enhanced, individual aspirations are fulfilled, and our cultural values and service to our communities are strengthened.

CULTURAL VALUES

1. **Teamwork**: We commit to working together to create a seamless and outstanding student experience

2. **Innovation**: We foster an environment that encourages creativity, taking considered risks, and driving progress to achieve goals.

3. **Health**: We contribute to active healthy living; striving to elevate our community's state of complete physical, mental, and social well-being.

4. **Commitment to Service**: We contribute to delivering high-quality programs and services.

5. **Continuous Improvement**: We commit to challenging ourselves and our colleagues to learn and grow.

6. **Accountability**: We accept responsibility for the consequences of our actions and decisions and those of our team.

SERVICE CREDO

Our passion for sport and active healthy living drives us to provide excellent service and to deliver a transformative experience with our customers.

SERVICE VALUES

1. **Reliable & Knowledgeable**: I take responsibility to know and enhance our facilities, services, policies, and culture.

2. **Personalized Attention**: I continuously seek to build relationships with our customers.

3. **Take Ownership**: I am accountable to our customers and take initiative as required to offer outstanding service.

4. **Pride in Facility**: I take pride in our facilities and contribute to a welcoming physical and social environment.

Like most innovations that are adopted in organizations, we always need people who lead the way. In this case, the Vikes Marketing and Engagement Team adopted coaching quicker than others and was able to show extended teams the difference that this kind of coaching could make. Most importantly, the team modeled the coaching themselves so others would get on board quickly.

As Rob McKay, the manager of the Marketing and Engagement Team, states about its use, "Most importantly, we had a coaching 'champion' within the team. I don't believe we would have been successful without Marlena Stubbings [the event manager] taking it on and leading us through the process. She is the real reason we are successful. Also, I had to buy in myself and actively participate in coaching as a manager. You have to model the behaviors you want to see in a team and coaching is no different. I've been coached by colleagues, student assistants, part-time and full-time staff. Coaching transcends hierarchical titles in my opinion."

Marlena highlights the role that coaching plays in building culture (the topic of Chapter 3). "Coaching creates more than a culture of service in a workplace; it builds and strengthens relationships in a work unit. Coaching has been key to the Vikes Marketing and Engagement Team coming together with trust and respect as a productive team that delivers excellent results."

In terms of keeping the momentum going, Rob adds, "We kept coaching top of mind by including 'coaching' as a standing item for all staff meetings. This is a round table report on staff experience with coaching. Great learning came from everyone's feedback."

In fact, Rob noted that the coaching has been more than he imagined. "One of our former employees applied for another position with another company [remember these are students looking for jobs at the end of their degrees] and during an interview asked the prospective employer, 'Do you have a coaching program?' The employer called us for a reference and also questioned us on the coaching program and the process. To me it highlights the value of coaching when it is important enough to be taken outside of the department walls."

Now the Marketing and Engagement Team use coaching in many different situations including email tone, presentations, leading meetings, and leading volunteers. Along the way, they made some excellent tools to help with the coaching, as well as a coaching framework that is used to run their coaching sessions. They also produced a one-page *cheat sheet* on coaching, and the Marketing and Engagement Team even developed a clear schedule of who is working with whom (see all of these below).

They have acted as a role model for other areas of Vikes and other teams have begun adopting an athletic approach to coaching in the organizational context. This case study shows that with persistence, a champion, the right tools, and modeling by the leaders, coaching becomes irresistible.

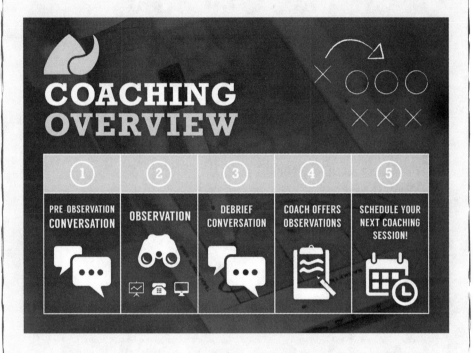

VIKES COACHING

WHY DO WE NEED COACHING?

Coaching is a process to support employees with their professional goals, facilitate service excellence, and improve the experience we create for our guests. Living and breathing excellence requires us to constantly ask how we can be better and work to improve our customer experience. Coaching is a proven tool that successful companies and organizations have adopted with great results.

WHAT DOES A COACHING SESSION LOOK LIKE?

A coaching session is when a 'coach' is tasked with observing a 'coachee' for 15-30 minutes while they are on the job. Following this, both parties take part in a debrief meeting where a 'coaching conversation' occurs. To be successful, coaching sessions need to be scheduled in advance. We encourage our staff to participate in at least two coaching sessions of 15-30 mins each month.

WHAT IS A COACHING CONVERSATION?

A 'coaching conversation' provides an opportunity for employee feedback and to explore challenges in an immediate and impactful way. A coaching conversation is reflective; it starts with open-ended questions from the coach to the coachee.

QUESTIONS TO ASK BEFORE OBSERVATION

→ What are your goals around service excellence?

→ What are your current challenges?

→ How are you working through those challenges?

QUESTIONS TO ASK AFTER OBSERVATION

→ What went well?

→ What was tricky?

→ What would you like to work on moving forward?

→ How can we better support you?

WHAT CAN WE HOPE TO GAIN FROM COACHING?

Coaching keeps service excellence front of mind. It facilitates discussion around our systems and procedures, reinforces our strengths and creates awareness around our challenges. Coaching is a tool that develops our staff, allows us to better understand and service our customer's needs, and creates a welcoming, efficient, and fun work environment at ATRS.

Marketing & Engagement Team Coaching Plan

Continue with weekly check-in meetings with supervisors (ALL).

Identify 2-3 professional goals for this semester that you would like to be coached on. These goals may evolve during the term.

Examples:

- Improve public speaking skills
- Communicate more effectively with coworkers
- Provide outstanding service to every guest and colleague

Within a coaching "buddy system" – schedule one coaching session each/month working your goals. Meet to determine focus and appropriate activities to observe. Switch coaching buddy each month.

Proposed Schedule:

September: Marlena-Bianca, Melissa-Rob, Ali –Jamie, Zac-Kevin, Erin-Gareth
October: Marlena-Gareth, Melissa-Bianca, Ali-Rob, Zac-Jamie, Erin-Kevin, Mira bye
November: Marlena-Mira, Melissa-Gareth, Ali-Bianca, Zac-Rob, Erin-Jamie, Kevin bye
December: Marlena-Jamie, Melissa-Kevin, Ali-MIra, Zac-Bianca, Erin-Rob

January: Marlena-Rob, Melissa-Jamie, Ali-Kevin, Zac-Mira, Erin-Bianca
February: Marlena-Melissa, Rob-Jamie, Ali-Zac, Kevin-Bianca, Erin-Zac
March: Marlena-Zac, Rob-Bianca, Ali-Erin, Melissa-Mira, Kevin-Jamie

Assessment:

We will include a coaching check-in as part of our M & E Team meetings.

Moment of Power 6:

The Moment You Adopt a Multi-dimensional Athletic Approach to Coaching Organizations

Building on Chapter 5, the next moment of power comes when the organization is able to adopt a multi-dimensional athletic approach to coaching by growing an employee's technical, mental, and physical skills.

Building Technical Skills

If we are to adopt an athletic approach to coaching in organizations, we must resist some of the coaching practices that occur in organizations at the present. To successfully build stronger technical skills in employees, we need to change our organizational coaching habits and become a lot more scientific with our approach.

In particular, I do not believe that coaching sessions that occur without using *data* are reliable. Coaching conversations that are based entirely on the coach's perception of the employee, without any data, or based solely the coachee's perception of their own behavior, are likely carried out with many misconceptions and biases (which were explored in Chapter 3).

Observation-Based Coaching

The best coaching sessions use observational based data. In the best-case scenario, although not always possible, this necessitates the coach witnessing the employee in their role.

When I say observe, I use the word observe in its broadest sense. That is, the observation could be based on hearing an employee, perhaps while they are running a teleconference or working in a call center serving the customer. Similarly, it could be reading a piece of work that the employee has done (a project proposal, for example) and providing feedback on that piece of written work. These are all objective observational data.

Further, the coach does not have to collect the data himself, as long as the data is credible and relevant, it can come from another source. For example, in Chapter 1 when I highlighted the research undertaken on coaching in the restaurant context, the coaching that occurred in those coaching sessions was undertaken by using the data through mystery shopping experiences.

So even though the coach was not the one to observe the server, the data is still credible and relevant; an independent party collected the data, which can still help employees see where they are.

A great example of the power of observation comes from Sir Alex Ferguson, the most successful soccer coach of all time. He recently published an article in the *Harvard Business Review* with Anita Elberse (2013).[122] In this article, he noted that as soon as he had become more observant as to what his players were doing, he was able to identify areas for them to improve so much more.

He states, "I don't think many people fully understand the value of observing. I came to see observation as a critical part of my management skills. The ability to see things is key—or, more specifically, the ability to see things you don't expect to see is key."

Ferguson began delegating training to his assistant coaches early in his career. Ferguson (2013) adds, "It was the best thing I ever did. It didn't take away my control. My presence and ability to supervise were always there, and what you can pick up by watching is incredibly valuable. Once I stepped out of the bubble, I became more aware of a range of details, and my performance level [as a coach] jumped."[123]

This is a very interesting concept because Ferguson is saying that you don't always have to be *the* coach. In fact, the best role you can play is the *head coach*, where you actually may coach from time to time, but often will use other people to help you coach. You can use their different perspective to fill in some of the blanks for the coachee and for you as the head coach. This head coach analogy means that you, as the coach, don't have to do *everything* for the employee.

Demonstration

Another potent way for a coach to grow someone's technical skills is by demonstrating the skill that they would like the employee to acquire. In accordance with social learning theory, athletic coaches usually demonstrate their knowledge by acting out or simulating the desired skill (modeling). Organizational coaches, however, do this much less frequently as noted in Chapter 5.

Leading by example and demonstration is recommended as a good way for the coachee to model behavior after the coach. In doing so, the coach could demonstrate effective behavior directly to the coachee. Albert Bandura (2000)[124] suggests that instructive modeling, as the first step, may aid in building self-efficacy.

A team leader demonstrating how to handle a frustrated customer, or a retail store manager demonstrating how an employee can build rapport with a customer in a face-to-face context, or a coachee watching the coach do a high-stakes presentation are three examples of how a coach can guide the employee in the right behaviors. These demonstrations also provide credibility to the leader who displays the technical skill he is trying to teach.

Very similar to this is *upward coaching*, where the employee coaches his team leader, for example, so that not only does the team leader demonstrate the skill they would like the employee to acquire, but also the team leader gets feedback as to how he can improve that particular skill, if appropriate. Importantly, upward coaching allows the leader to show vulnerability that she is willing to put it all on the line, and to be coached as well. This is an excellent modeling strategy.

Practice

Another way to grow a technical skill in an organizational context would be to allocate practice time for the employee to grow that skill. This, of course, is something that athletes do all the time and was identified in Chapter 5 in terms of how to grow your expertise as one of the three crucial ways to grow your expertise—deliberate practice.

In an organizational context, this requires the coach to ensure that the employee commits to a particular work plan at the end of the coaching session, and work out how they will practice that particular skill between now and the next coaching session. Without this commitment to practice at the end of the coaching session, there is unlikely to be any technical change in the employee skills. Chapter 7 outlines a coaching model where commitment is gained at the end of the coaching session.

Obviously, this is not like athletics; employees cannot endlessly take time away from work to practice deliberately. Most athletes spend much of their time in practice and little time *performing*. Employees, however, have to spend most of their time on stage working for an internal or external customer. Allowing them to practice off-line for large amounts of time clearly is not possible. Much of this practice time, then, has to happen in real time (i.e., where the employees are actually working). This means we need to create a safe environment for them to practice the skills and encourage them to take risks, but manage these risks carefully.

Consider a salesperson that is learning the technical skill of doing a customer-need analysis, where they go through a questioning session, carefully understanding the customer's needs and then recommending products and services that meet their needs after they fully understand what their customer's requirements are. Clearly, we cannot allow salespeople six months of off-line practice before they get this right in front of the customer, but we should allow practice time to role-play this technique with an expert, team leader, or another employee, and ensure they spend time observing other salespeople so that their practice can be more deliberate.

At some stage, however, you do have to let the salesperson practice with a real customer (as opposed to an inflatable one, which is no fun, I find) as there's only so much practice that can happen in mock preparation. This is the opportunity for leaders to observe the employees and provide much-needed feedback early on in the process. Overall, carving out practice time can be tough in organizations, but opportunities for practice always help move the employee toward perfection.

No athlete—not even an amateur—would consider performing without practice time, yet organizations rarely allow their employees hands-on practice, role-plays, or simulations. This practice time could well be the difference between moving from good to great.

One observation I have had is that coaching gets reversed in organizations compared to athletics. In athletics those at the bottom of the pyramid demand coaching less. For example, amateur athletes might practice a few hours a week, while semi-professional or professional athletes spend many, many hours practicing and often have multiple coaches (Roger Federer has, like, 27 coaches).

To the contrary, in organizations I find resistance grows as employees move up the corporate ladder. Front-line employees are often the keenest to be coached, but as you move up to team-leaders, managers, directors, etc., they think they have *made it* so demand less coaching or even oppose it. ("Really? me? Coaching is for those lower down as they don't have what it takes yet.")

Of course, this makes no sense because as employees get more senior the stakes are higher, just as they are for a professional athlete. This is a great example of a fixed mindset. Remember Eric Schmidt[125] from Chapter 1—he resisted coaching because he was the CEO of Google (I've made it!) but then realized the difference it made and now is a huge advocate for it.

High-Quality and Timely Feedback

Another way of growing someone's technical skills is by offering feedback— where the coach identifies whether or not the coachee is on the path to acquiring a particular skill or if changes still need to be made.

Again, as we noted in Chapter 5, most feedback occurs very irregularly (e.g., in the annual performance review or without context). In these cases the employee does not realize they're even being coached. This feedback is neither timely nor useful.

High-quality feedback is based on systematically identifying opportunities to give regular feedback to the employees so they know they are making progress (and we've already identified the power of making progress earlier in this book) or the changes they need to make to build further progress. In this case, the feedback must be at the earliest opportunity so the employee feels like she is on the right track. In these instances, consistent—versus irregular—coaching sessions make all the difference in the world.

The table below summarizes the different coaching tactics for developing technical skills based on using an athletic approach to coaching in organizations.

Table 6-1: Five Coaching Tactics for Technical Skills

1.	Coach observes coachee performing in their role.
2.	When a new skill or technique is introduced, the coach does a good job at demonstrating it.
3.	Coach gives regular time to coachee so employee can practice new skills.
4.	Coach gives feedback at the earliest opportunity to the coachee, rather than waiting for formal job evaluations.
5.	Coach gives valuable performance feedback.

Mental Skills

The second dimension of athletic coaching that needs to be developed further in organizations is the need to grow the employees' mental skills. As noted in Chapter 5, during our comparison of sports coaching and organizational coaching, there is very little mental skill development in employees through coaching. Michael Read (2011) discovered in his interviews with many organizational coaches that "…many did not feel as though psychological arousal management was part of the coach's role."[126]

Read, Colgate, Tax, and Corwin, for example, suggest in their paper, "Skills in the sport psychology tradition, such as self-talk and refocusing, and physiological skills, such as progressive relaxation and meditation, offer incredible opportunities [for businesses]."[127] As Coleman Griffith (2007) states, "Most successful coaches are psychologists of no small ability."[128] The organizational coach can dedicate time and resources to mental skills training, which may enable the coachees to perform under pressure, tackle obstacles and persist, narrow their focus of attention and absorption in an activity, and better manage their determination.[129]

Critically, mental training can enable employees to maintain a continual growth mindset, which is so important to career growth.[130] To ensure employees are focused on skill development, coaches must get coachees to remind themselves that expertise comes from deliberate practice and is not an innate skill. Visualization of achieving career goals and self-talk in tough situations can remind employees that they *can* reach their goals and stop the fixed mindset from dominating.

Coaches who understand the field of performance psychology and understand how decision making, beliefs, images, and feelings affect and are affected by performance are invaluable. Cleary, this is training that organizations can provide their coaches as they develop a coaching system—outlined in Chapter 2.

Coaches utilize their mental expertise to assist coachees in developing their ability to be focused, determined, committed, and confident in the workplace. The development of psychological skills requires a systematic coaching program designed to utilize the employees' strengths, while also addressing weaknesses, so as to remain focused on achieving targeted goals, even in the face of unexpected challenges (which all organizations repeatedly face).

We will now examine three areas of mental skill training—managing goals, inspiring the coachee by showing them you believe in them, and helping the coachee improve their mental focus.

Goal-Setting

Goal-setting theory is one of the most influential theories of employee motivation. In fact, in a survey of organizational behavior scholars, it has been rated as *the* most important theory (out of 73 theories).[131] The theory has been supported in over 1,000 studies with employees ranging from blue-collar workers to research-and-development employees, and there is robust support that setting goals is connected to employee performance developments.[132] The theory is simple: When a coach helps employees to set goals, the research shows that the employees will raise their performance, in contrast to those employees who don't have a coach urging them to set goals.

In order to motivate employees, goals should be specific, measurable, achievable, relevant, and time-bound (SMART). Employees will not be motivated by simply having a goal. Think about all the New Year's resolutions you've made and how many of those you've stuck to. The high failure rate of these goals comes mainly because they are not SMART goals. SMART goals motivate coachees because they energize behavior, give it direction, provide a challenge, force employees to think outside the box, and devise new and novel methods of performing.

Goals are more effective in motivating employees when employees receive feedback on their accomplishments and are committed to goals. Badly devised goals can be negative because they hamper learning, can cause a single-minded pursuit of goals at the expense of other activities, and maybe even encourage unethical behavior. It's the goal—not just the goal setting—that is key. A coach can work to help set appropriate and meaningful goals.

Effective goals are specific and measurable. If goals are not specific and measurable, how would you know whether or not you have reached the goal? Without specific goals, a wide variance of performance levels could potentially be acceptable. For the same reason, "do your best" is not an effective goal because it is not measurable and does not give you a specific target.

Certain aspects of performance are easier to quantify. For example, it is relatively easy to set specific goals for productivity, sales, number of errors, or absenteeism. However, some measures are harder to obtain. For example, at Commonwealth Bank of Australia, a key metric for the insurance side of the organization was customers' perceptions of claims handling. This was a softer metric that we did not have access to internally, but was, obviously, critical for us to go out and collect.

The science of achievement goals shows that the coach needs to find a balance between goals that are stretch goals, but not too hard. Clearly, if the goals are too hard for the coachees, they will become disillusioned with the coaching process. Interestingly though, even easy goals are ineffective. In fact, in the many seminars I've taught on coaching, the one thing I often hear is that great coaches are able to get coachees to grow in areas the employee never believed possible. That is because coaches pushed them to excel. By believing in them and pushing them beyond their limits, they achieved success beyond their original expectations.

According to a Hay Group study, one factor that distinguishes companies that are ranked as "Most Admired Companies" in *Fortune* magazine is that they set more difficult goals.[133] Put simply, easy goals don't set a challenge for the coachee.

Finally, effective goals are relevant and time bound. They are relevant in that the employees see that these goals will grow them in ways they think are meaningful to them, and they also see how they are connected to organizational goals. Also, effective goals contain a statement regarding when the proposed goal will be reached. For example, "increasing sales to a region by 8 percent by March of the next fiscal year" gives employees a sense of time urgency. Again, the role of the coach is to ensure that the goals that the employees are setting are in line in all of the above ways. In many ways coaches need to become experts at helping employees to set goals because the evidence of the difference they make is unquestionable.

There are two further conditions that contribute to goal effectiveness (once goals have been set).[134] First, the coachee must receive feedback on progress toward the stated goals. Providing employees with quantitative figures about their sales, growing customer satisfaction, or other metrics is useful for feedback purposes. However, the coach may be able to spot progress in particular areas that relates to the goals through the continual coaching sessions and even feedback that identifies, qualitatively, that they are growing and improving.

Second, the employee must commit to the goals that have been set. As a testament to the importance of goal commitment, Microsoft actually calls employee goals *commitments*.[135] Goal commitment refers to the degree to which a person is dedicated to reaching the goal. Research shows that when individuals have a supportive and trust-based relationship with the coach, goal commitment tends to be higher. Similarly, when the coach ensures that the coachee participates fully in the goal setting process, the coach is more likely to be committed, too.[136] After all, whose ideas do you like the most? Your own or someone else's? Overall, when you can participate in the goal setting process, you take ownership of the goals.

In summary, goal setting, feedback toward the goals, and goal commitment from the coachee are key tasks the coach must master to ensure the employee has focused goals that steer him to be a success within the organization.

The Coach Encourages, Believes, and Connects With the Coachee

One of the amazing things coaches can do for employees is to believe in them. Over and over again, I hear in the seminars that I teach that the best coaches are the ones who believe in the people they coach. When this happens, then employees are far more inspired to achieve their goals and grow in their respective fields, whether this is in sports or in an organizational context. Believing in the coachee is the second way, after setting meaningful goals, to drive the mental skills of the employee.

When a coach believes in us, we entertain possibilities that stretch the limits of our own thinking. Part of this involves building the coachee up rather than knocking him down; great coaches always build self-esteem rather than undermine it.

A coach who is authentic, who always turns up to coaching sessions, and demonstrates that they have the employee's best interests at heart are indeed the best coaches, regardless of how long they have been coaching. This is far better than an experienced coach who has lost interest in their coachees.

The Coach Provides Strategies to Improve the Coachee's Mental Focus

Finally, a good coach can help the coachee grow mentally by providing explicit strategies to improve the coachee's mental focus, particularly in high-stakes situations. As noted earlier, some of the most successful strategies that athletes use are visualization, self-talk, and simulations.

Visualization is defined as using imagery to see the outcomes you want to occur and learn to deal with them before they occur.[137] Robin Vealey and Christy Greenleaf (2001) define imagery as a "mental technique that programs the mind and body to perform optimally."[138]

Effective imagery is used to increase coachee motivation and attention control while decreasing performance anxiety.[139] Bruce Peltier[140] (2011) reports on lessons from athletic coaches by concluding, "Virtually all successful athletic coaches use covert imagery rehearsal, or visualization."[141] Visualization is also mentioned[142] as a technique used in both sport and business with some anecdotal success.

Self-talk involves the use of mood triggering words and positive self-statements repeated to gain concentration, which should be positive-oriented statements.[143] Another mental skill involves reframing self-talk by turning negatives into positives.[144] Obviously, employees will not use self-talk all the time, but in a high-stakes sales meeting, before a presentation, or negotiations, then self-talk may be useful.

Finally, simulation is a great way for employees to gain mental focus. Simulation is about mimicking real life context so that employees can understand what it could be like to be in that situation. Simulation is often used in situations like negotiations so that employees can understand the possible mental context in which this activity will occur. Obviously, simulations are good for technical training, too.

Table 6-2: Five Coaching Tactics for Mental Skills

1	The coach helps the coachee set goals.
2	The coach helps the coachee evaluate goal progress through feedback.
3	The coach obtains goal commitment from coachee.
4	The coach encourages, believes, and connects with the coachee.
5	The coach provides strategies to improve the coachee's mental focus.

Case Study:
A Virtual Approach to Athletic Coaching at TELUS

I spoke with Jeffrey Puritt, President & CEO at TELUS International, the fastest growing part of TELUS, which is the leading telecommunications company in Canada. TELUS International is TELUS' global arm, providing a global contact center and business process outsourcing services to corporations in the telecommunications, utilities, high tech, gaming, finance, retail, e-commerce, travel and logistics, and health care industries. TELUS International has delivery centers in Canada, the United States, Europe, Central America, and Asia.

The growth of TELUS International has been incredible. Started in 2005, the company already has 22,000 employees with delivery centers in eight countries, serving customers in over 35 languages. In May 2016, TELUS sold 35 percent of TELUS International. This stake valued TELUS International at approximately $1 billion dollars, which highlights how successful TELUS International has been.

According to Jeff, "Coaching has played an important role in my career (and life) and I have strived to ensure that we continue to make coaching readily available to our high-performing team members at TELUS International. I cannot overstate the importance of having someone knowledgeable, experienced, honest, and candid serve as a guide, as a sounding board, to help support all our leaders' continued development."

Jeff further added, "We are always looking to innovate with coaching with leaders and our front-line team members. We know that on-going coaching drives team member engagement and productivity, and our team member engagement scores [TELUS International's engagement score, as measured by Aon Hewitt, is at 80 percent, which is amazing for a predominantly contact-center environment] and business results are a reflection of that innovative approach to coaching."

A good example of this innovation is the Ignite coaching simulation game, which is used across TELUS. TELUS uses an athletic approach to coaching to teach high potential leaders about their culture, values, and important leadership competencies. In this way coaching is being used to drive organizational goals of better leadership and execution of corporate strategy.

TELUS created Ignite as a coaching tool so employees could learn about and deploy the TELUS Leadership Philosophy and its 11 leadership competencies, which represent the key skills that align its values and support behaviors that elevate and differentiate employee performance.

TELUS partnered with gaming company Ncite Factory to bring this idea to life. With existing TELUS leaders and high potential employees in mind, they set out to design a game in which employees could practice their leadership and coaching skills and behaviors in a virtual, simulated role play environment. After two years of development, the collaboration produced TELUS Ignite Speed Skating (Ignite)—one of three gamification applications at TELUS today.

Ignite represents a game-like coaching application that enables employees to develop their ability to think about technical ability development, mental skills of the coachee, and their energy through the powerful vehicle of the coach/athlete metaphor. In order to perform well in the game, the coaches must be attentive to their athlete's personalities (mental skills) and constantly be adjusting their leadership style to ensure the greatest impact on both individual and team performance. Using algorithms and decision trees, every in-game action is mapped back to one of TELUS' 11 leadership competencies, with instant feedback provided to the player to either reinforce or course correct. Below is a picture of the game in action.

Every two weeks the coach and his athlete travel to a regional race where the leaders compete with other TELUS leaders to test their skills as a coach. Success depends on how well the coach uses the TELUS leadership philosophies and adapts their coaching skills to grow their athletes. At the end you get ranked against the other *head coaches* so you can see how you did and earn bragging rights, and winners get to make a donation to the charity of their choice! The idea is that this game helps TELUS leaders on the path to mastery by seeing themselves as coaches. The role of feedback is clear; the TELUS leaders use feedback to help their coachees grow and they in turn get feedback from the game as to how they are doing.

Since TELUS Ignite went live in June 2013, over 250 leaders from different business units, roles, and levels have participated in the simulation. Player feedback and results to date have been very positive, and there is a strong interest from the business to leverage this innovative learning application for other talent development activities.

With the introduction of Ignite, TELUS is leading the way in executing an athletic approach to coaching inside an organization. It is a game-based coaching tool that teaches culture, values, and behaviors as the base content to help employees improve on their leadership skills, teamwork, creativity, problem solving, and other important aspects of personal and interpersonal development.

As Jeff Puritt reminds us, we must innovate with coaching (Joey Restaurant Group and Delta Dental were great examples of innovation in coaching, too) as much as we do in other organizational areas, and Ignite is a great example of this innovation in action.

Random Story #6: Mental Focus through Music

10 Most Enjoyable Activities	
Activities	**Score**
1. Listening to music	4.81
2. Playing with children	4.81
3. Attending sports event	4.74
4. Hunting, fishing, boating, hiking	4.73
5. Parties or reception	4.72
6. Purchase personal service	4.43
7. General out-of-time leisure	4.39
8. Cafe or bar	4.39
9. Sports or exercise	4.26
10. Worship or religious act	4.24

This is cool. Really cool. Gallup asked 350,000 people from 150 countries what their most enjoyable activities were. Listening to music came out on top. Number one. It just beat out "playing with children" by a third decimal place. Playing with children would have come out on top, except those people with kids voted it as one of the least enjoyable activities.

Listening to music is amazing, isn't it? It can change our mood, make us want to dance, bring back fond memories, and even get us to fall in love (although not on a Monday morning, I find).

But, you will notice that music didn't get a perfect score. That's because music doesn't always work out in the way it is supposed to. Remember being at a club, and they didn't play the music you want and it ruined your night, or you chose the wrong karaoke song…you know what I mean.

Anyway, it happens to us all. Recently, in my class, I asked my students to pick a song that represented the topic I was teaching at the time. They chose "Are You Gonna Go My Way" by Lennie Kravitz, when I was teaching strategy as an example.

However, after choosing a song for the topic of the class every week for about eight weeks, they got bored and started choosing songs with filthy lyrics that I'd never heard of. The chosen song would be played in class and, unknowingly, I would play one minute of the disgusting words (e.g., "Like a Boss" by SNL), which had the students in fits. Let's say the activity stopped relatively quickly after that.

The best unfortunate music story I have heard is about my wife's friend who was getting married in Ireland a few years ago. Okay, so it was 1991. Anyway, this lady wanted a romantic song to be played as she was walking down the aisle at the end of the ceremony. So she went to the organist, who was an elderly gentleman, and asked him to play the theme from *Robin Hood*.

Now, she meant Bryan Adams' "(Everything I Do) I Do It for You," the theme song from the *Robin Hood* movie starring Kevin Costner. The song was number one in the UK and Ireland for about six months at the time of the wedding. Now, if you don't know this song you must pick up your phone, go to YouTube, and listen to the first minute. It's very romantic, feel free, right now, to grab the person nearest to you and smooch.

Anyway, the organist said, "Sure, I can play that song." Now, she was quite skeptical that he knew this song because the organist was old and this song was modern, but she went with it because she was extremely busy preparing for the wedding and had many other things to worry about.

So, the wedding is over and they prepare to walk down the aisle and leave the church to a very romantic song. Unfortunately, she should have listened to her gut because the organist was very old and the only Robin Hood theme tune he knew was from the 1950s (which again you need to listen to really get the flavor of—search these exact words on YouTube and listen: "Theme Song to *The Adventures of Robin Hood*").

The song goes like this: "[trumpets at the beginning] Robin Hood, Robin Hood, riding through the glen. Robin Hood, Robin Hood with his band of men. Feared by the bad, loved by the good. Robin Hood, Robin Hood, Robin Hood." Now you must sing it *really fast* to get the full effect.

Anyway, actually I don't know the end of the story and how they reacted. I just hope they played their part and stole wallets and watches from the rich people in the expensive seats in the church and gave them to the poor people sitting at the back. I smile when I think that may have happened.

Music—sometimes it bites us!

Physical Skills

The final dimension of adopting an athletic approach to coaching in organizations is helping to ensure employees have energy at work. While some organizations have taken this approach very seriously, many do not see it as part of their role as an employer.

Read (2011),[145] for example, interviewed 62 athletic coaches. Seventy-nine percent of them reported that they involved themselves in the coachee's physical fitness either "often" or "always" as part of their coaching. In terms of organizational coaches, 53 were interviewed, and only 8 percent reported being involved in their coachee's physical fitness. Read summarizes his discussions by stating, "Organizational coaches reported rarely being involved in a coachee's physical fitness—and usually only when first mentioned by the coachee. Several organizational coaches indicated that if the issue were presented, they would help the coachee identify goals or appropriate activities to address the concern."[146] This was almost entirely a reactive activity from organizational coaches. The research discovered very similar results for hydration, nutrition, injury prevention, and physical testing—athletics coaches used this extensively in their coaching practices but organizational coaches used it rarely.

Of course, this is not a fair comparison. Athletes need to be in the best physical shape to perform, whereas employees in organizations do not. But we should not brush off this opportunity. As Read (2011) notes, nearly 50 percent of workplace injuries originate from falls, strenuous movements, and overexertion.[147] In order of prevalence, the top five injuries causing lost workdays were muscle strains, back strains, fractures, occupational diseases, and contusions.[148]

Organizational coaches who ignore the physical side of coaching are missing an opportunity for a more complete approach to coaching in organizations, and should consider using it more extensively. It seems clear that an employee who has energy at work will be a happier, higher performing employee. Many researchers[149] suggest that energy is an employee's most important resource and fundamental to high performance. Put simply, an employee who has poor work and life balance, or an employee who has poor health through lack of education and coaching in this area is an employee who is unlikely to give her best at work.

Of course, some organizational leaders argue that it is not their job to monitor or discuss physical health…employees are adults and should manage their own health and fitness levels.

With this line of logic, however, why then wouldn't this be the case for career management as well? Why can't employees manage their own careers, and why would they need assistance in setting goals or intervention with regard to growing their abilities? If this were the sole responsibility of the employee—knowing the areas they want to grow and achieve success in their career—why would we need to provide coaching for them so they can advance their career?

To be more successful, organizational coaches could educate employees on healthy living, how to be safer at work, and how to manage stress. Organizational coaches have access to resources and knowledge on health issues that employees often don't have. Likewise, the coach could provide access to other specialists as well. In short, great coaches see the person they are coaching as a whole person rather than just looking at them as an employee who needs to advance their technical skills so they can help leaders achieve organizational goals.

Twitter is great example of a company that takes physical fitness seriously. The social media giant encourages its 1,000 employees at the San Francisco headquarters to stay healthy by offering onsite yoga, Pilates, and CrossFit classes. Onsite massages and acupuncture sessions are also available for a fee.

"The attitude and energy we all bring to work are so important to our culture," says Amy Obana, HR and Wellness program manager at Twitter. "But such energy can make us susceptible to fatigue and burnout. Twitter aims to avoid this by offering diverse fitness and wellness programs to encourage renewal so that as employees we can manage our energy better and get more done in a sustainable way."[150]

Another example is Progressive Insurance. Headquartered in Cleveland, Ohio, this insurance company helps its 25,000 employees stay healthy with an onsite Fitness Center, Weight Watchers reimbursement program, yoga and boot camp classes, personal training, and a smoking cessation program.[151]

"These amenities show Progressive's commitment to employees and their daily desire to be productive both in work and life," says Pamela Sraeel, senior manager of Benefit Services. Sraeel says making a healthy lifestyle more convenient and affordable for employees has resulted in a more motivated and less stressed staff. "When employees are healthy, they feel good. They innovate, solve problems, and take initiative, which is imperative in a tough global marketplace,"[152] she says.

Coaching for Physical Skills

Given that we see some organizations interested in promoting physical fitness and health inside organizations, while others are generally reluctant for their organizational coaches to get involved in this activity, the question is how should coaches go about coaching people so they are safe, healthy, and have energy at work?

This is where the notion of the head coach, which we introduced earlier in this chapter, becomes important. It is unlikely that most people who were coaching in an organizational context have been trained to offer competent health advice. Also think about how uncomfortable that would be on a one-to-one basis. ("Excuse me, but you are looking a little bit overweight, and I have noticed you've grown over the last few months of our coaching sessions. Can I offer some dietary advice?")

There are a few ways this can work, however. The first is team-based coaching. In this scenario, a coach provides education and advice to the team as a whole rather than singling out one particular person. The coach might organize health events for the team such as yoga sessions, health seminars by specialists (perhaps to discuss hydration in the workplace, or correct posture while sitting at the desk), and create team-based competitions (e.g., who can walk the most steps in the week), with the winner getting a health-related prize (rather than a large slice of cake). Or where the team can achieve a particular goal such as walk 100,000 combined steps in a particular week and ensure that some of this activity occurs during work time so employees are taking healthy breaks.

Second, as the head coach, the organizational coach can ensure that any health benefits provided by the organization are shared with the coachees. For example, reminding employees what exactly their health benefits are, reminding them of opportunities for free massages, gym memberships, free annual checkups, etc. This is a great way to share with employees all the benefits that are available to them, and a great way to promote a healthy work environment.

Finally, in the role of head coach, you could point individual employees toward specific health specialists, for example, giving coachees access to physiotherapists, chiropractors, or therapists where appropriate.

A major part of health in the workplace is work/life balance: managing stress in an employee and staying relaxed at work. Again, remember how difficult it is for an athlete to perform if he is burned out when going to perform.

While some may think this form of coaching should fall under the *mental skills* of coaching, the reality is that the first signs of stress and burn out are physical signs: they cannot sleep properly, their eating habits become erratic, or their health begins to decline, and it manifests in headaches, constant sickness, and other related symptoms, such as chest pains and tense muscles.

If the coach understands that the physical side of the workplace is important, the more they will educate themselves in this area and provide the right education and advice for the coachee.

The table below outlines the five coaching tactics coaches can use to promote physical skills in the organization. I believe this is an emerging area in organizations and particularly for organizational coaching. Coaches who coach employees on the technical, mental, and physical skills really are taking coaching a step further because they are viewing the employee as a complete person and thinking about everything they can do to help the coachee develop mastery.

Table 6-3: Five Coaching Tactics for Physical Skills

1	A good coach improves a coachee's physical fitness.
2	A good coach improves the coachee's ability to stay relaxed and manage stress.
3	A good coach improves the coachee's ability to prevent injuries.
4	A good coach helps the coachee to have healthy eating habits.
5	A good coach encourages the coachee to stay hydrated.

The seventh chapter in this book takes Chapters 5 and 6 a step farther: How do we actually execute these approaches in on-going coaching sessions?

We need to know exactly how to run a great coaching session and what the mechanics of a great coaching session are. We can be the most skilled coach in the world, have the right mindset, and always turn up to the coaching sessions, but if we don't manage each coaching session expertly, then we will never get the most out of organizational coaching. In the next chapter, we will discuss the seventh moment of power—the moment you run a powerful, and very delicious, coaching session.

Moment of Power 7:
The Moment You Run an Effective Coaching Session Using Fair Process

Now that we have reached Chapter 7, let's have a look at the coaching session itself. It may seem like madness that it has taken six chapters to get to the ins and outs of an actual coaching session, but everything we have done to this point is critical; creating a system, training for the growth mindset, adopting an athletic approach to coaching, and understanding the psychology behind coaching. The more these aspects are designed into the coaching process, the more effective the coaching sessions will be. (I do realize, of course, that these last few sentences were probably obvious, and that I likely have had this discussion entirely with myself.)

Chapter 6 took an in-depth look at the outcomes we hope to achieve through coaching. We are looking to grow the coachee's technical, mental, and physical skills so that they grow into an expert. This three-dimensional approach is all about high-quality feedback in the right areas that the employee needs to grow.

However, those outcomes only occur after an effective coaching process. To create an effective coaching process we look at the science of *fair process*. Even when reaching an outcome that we desire, the process is often just as important—if not more important—than the outcome.

That is, if the coach manages to help the coachee acquire technical skills, for example, the way the coach manages the process may discourage the coachee from ever wanting to be coached again. For example, the coach may neglect to ask the coachee's opinion in terms of the skills that are being focused upon in the coaching session. Or, perhaps the coach periodically cancels the coaching sessions, which suggests that the coaching isn't that important after all.

Research[153] has established that people care as much about the fairness of the process through which an outcome is produced as they do about the outcome itself. Other researchers[154] have demonstrated the power of fair process across diverse cultures and social settings.

Chan Kim and Renée Mauborgne, the authors of *Blue Ocean Strategy*, the uber famous strategy book, state, "Fair process responds to a basic human need. All of us, whatever our role in a company, want to be valued as human beings and not as "personnel" or "human assets." We want others to respect our intelligence. We want our ideas to be taken seriously. And, we want to understand the rationale behind specific decisions. People are sensitive to the signals conveyed through a company's decision-making processes. Such processes can reveal a company's willingness to trust people and seek their ideas—or they can signal the opposite."[155]

Procedural fairness is activated in the coaching context by:[156] 1) the completeness of information collected by the coach, including the coachee's opportunity to add to the information, 2) the coach's use of the information, and 3) the extent to which coachees believe they can influence the outcome.[157]

Research into a framework for fair process has come from many areas. The three main domains that have developed the role that fair processes can play are business, law, and education. In education, they have used the fair process model to help instructors teach students effectively. In law, fair process is used to describe judicial proceedings that are conducted in such a manner as to conform to fundamental concepts of justice and equality. In business, the fair process model has been used to enable the leaders to engage in constructive discussions with the employees, rather than just making decisions without hearing their voice.

After investigating a number of fair process frameworks,[158] I created the model below. This framework works in organizations I have worked with and represents a pragmatic approach for use of a research-based, scientific framework. The five stages of the fair process are outlined below.

Figure 7-1: Fair Process Coaching Model

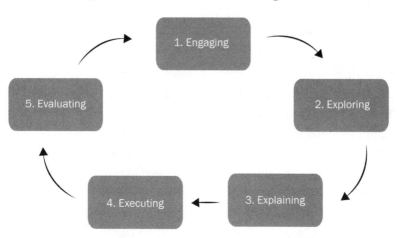

Engaging: This first step is all about framing. This means engaging the coachee in conversation about what can be expected of the coaching session. The more the coachee is involved in the framing, the more effective the coaching session will be. If the coachee is given a seat at the table, they feel like they own the coaching sessions and likely will be more engaged. This helps ensure the fair process they seek. Below are some powerful questions related to the first step of engagement:

- What skills do you need to improve upon to do your current job?

- What are some of your biggest roadblocks to moving forward?

- What strengths do you have that you'd like to utilize?

- What's important and what do you value in your role?

- What engages and excites you in your current role?

- What are you passionate about?

- What skills would help you better align with your goals and the firm's goals?

- What have you been doing to prepare yourself to move ahead in your career?

Exploring: This part of the coaching session is when the actual coaching occurs. Here, the coach and the coachee explore opportunities for growth. This could even be an observation session, for example, with feedback occurring at the end of the session.

In the explore stage, to ensure the coachees own their coaching, it is important that they try to identify, wherever possible, their own opportunities for improvement and growth, rather than being directed by the coach. Again in the fair process context, when the coachees can identify opportunities for improvement, they are more likely to buy into their coaching plan and see the coaching sessions as equitable. How committed will coachees be if their coach is constantly telling them what to do next? Consider some of the questions that may be used in the explore stage:

- Based on this coaching situation, what is not working as well as you would like?

- Based on this coaching situation, what do you need to do differently?

- What makes this situation challenging?

- How might others see this situation?

- How might you have contributed to this situation?

- What impact is this having on you? On others (your team/peers)?

- What are the consequences if the current situation does not change?

- How does this influence your goals?

Explaining: This is where coaching could go from nondirective to directive. As stated above, in the explore stage, wherever possible, the coachee is encouraged to own the execute stage of the coaching process by identifying the things that had gone well, the things that were difficult, and any areas where improvement can be made. However, when the coach can identify things that the coachee cannot see, the coach needs to move into the directive phase and point out to the coachee opportunities for growth.

The critical point here is that the coachees are much more likely to listen to the view of the coach and see these insights as fair if the coachees have had a chance to discover many of the possible explanations for themselves (which should happen in the explore stage). Below are some powerful questions around the explain phase:

- Could I share my perceptions of what worked well, or was difficult, and what you could do differently?

- How does this fit with what you think is happening?

- Am I seeing this in the right way or did I misinterpret the situation?

- Which comments of mine do you agree with?

- Which comments of mine do you disagree with?

At this point, it is critical to realize the importance of the transition between explore to explain. If the explore step is done too quickly, and the coachees do not feel they are given enough time to reflect on their situation, then it is unlikely that they will be listening very closely when it comes to the explaining stage, which is the directive part of the coaching model. It is often desirable to skip the explain stage completely if the coachees are fully aware of what needs to happen next, and/or you really need for the coachees to work it out for themselves.

However, in those situations where you *do* want to move into the explaining phase, the exercise below is a fantastic way to manage that transition. This makes a great visual exercise when you are teaching coaching inside organizations. The exercise is very straightforward.

Exercise

Call someone out of the audience and run a mock coaching session with them. Obviously, this person needs to be briefed beforehand. You then explain this fictional situation to the audience. (It's even better if you know a member of the audience really well so that you could create a real-life situation.)

With two glasses of water, you then represent what would happen if you only used directive coaching. With both glasses two-thirds full, you, as the coach, start to explain to the coachee what you thought was done well in the coaching session, what was tricky, and what should be done differently next time. With each comment, you add water from your glass into the coachee's glass. As you go through these three parts of the feedback, the coachee's glass of water gets fuller and fuller. By the time you reach the fifth comment, the glass starts to overflow and spills onto the floor. This represents a brain that is filled with far too much information.

The coach needs to make an opportunity for the coachee to empty his head and reflect. Instead, with information overload, the coachee finds it difficult to listen to the information and absorb what is being shared. By the time the coach gets to the third area, where improvements can be made, the coachee is likely to shut down completely, especially if he hasn't participated in the give and take of the conversation.

Once you have demonstrated the overflowing cup of water and you have had industrial cleaners come and clean up the mess, you can then do this example **again,** but in this case you get the coachee to start by saying what was done well. In this scenario the coachee begins filling up your glass of water from his.

After the coachee has explored what was believed to be done well, what was tricky, and what could be done differently (stating one insight from each area), it is the coach's turn. Because the coachee has stated a lot of what the coach was going to say, and the coachee's glass is only about half-full, when the coach gives his insights, the coachee's glass never overfills, and the coachee has plenty of headspace to listen.

The idea is to demonstrate that in this example of fair process, the coachee is always listening because he has had a chance to empty his mind before the coach's thoughts were shared.

Random Story #7: When Words are Misinterpreted

Of course, feedback in the English-language context requires sidestepping many bombs in terms of the misinterpretation of what you are saying. There are so many words and phrases in the English language that can be misconstrued. For example, we had a builder come round recently, as we were thinking of turning a large bedroom into a bedroom with an en suite, and the builder talked about starting the project by separating out the two rooms by putting up drywall. I looked to him quizzically and said, "I didn't know having a wet wall was an option." This builder decided that we were rubbish clients, and we had to find someone else.

My favorite story about the fatality of the English language concerns a friend of mine who was invited round their boss' house for dinner. My friend's boss was a woman who was incredible at what she did and, in this case, her husband stayed at home and raised the kids and did all of the cooking. It turned out to be a very awkward evening, as my friend really didn't get on well with the husband, who he often found to be quite annoying in previous encounters. This time was no different. Disaster struck when it came to the main course, the husband was serving out pieces of chicken and he said to my friend, "How many pieces of chicken would you like?"

My friend said, "Just one."

The husband replied, "Well, there is no need to be polite."

So, my friend said, "Okay, just one, you idiot."

Let's just say my friend wasn't working in that company much longer.

My point here is that the English language is full of potholes, so be careful with the feedback you give in coaching sessions because it can always be taken the wrong way!

How to Ensure the Coach and Coachee Share in the Coaching Conversation

Here is another way to think about ensuring both the coach and coachee have their say in a coaching session.

1. "Let's start with your perspective of the [fill in the blank]. **What do you think worked well in that coaching session?**"

2. Ask, "**What was tricky for you?**"

3. Ask, "**What would you do differently next time?**"

4. Once the employee has given his perspective, you know whether the feedback you are about to give is similar to his perception, and how sensitive you need to be about your feedback. What is important is that the coachee has *dumped* his thoughts and is ready to take in additional thoughts from you. Ask, "**Would you like some feedback from me?**"

5. Tell them **what you think was done well.**

6. Tell them **what you think was tricky.**

7. Tell them **what you think should be done differently** next time.

8. BOOM!

Executing: The fourth stage of the fair process coaching model is where the coachees make a plan as to how they will *execute* on the opportunities for improvement—those that were discovered in the coaching session.

The whole idea of coaching is that the coachee works on the areas identified in the coaching session between coaching sessions. If they don't own that plan they are unlikely to commit to that plan. Again this is where SMART goals are important, because the more the coachees are committed to executing the plan (because they had a major role in identifying the opportunities for improvement and creating the plan) the more likely they are to execute that plan. Below are the powerful questions on the executing step of fair process:

- What could we learn from this situation/problem/issue?

- Is your plan SMART? (Specific, measurable, attainable, realistic, and time bound?)

- How will you make the time to practice the things we identified in this coaching session?

- How can the organization support you going forward to help you execute successfully?

- What can you control in this situation? What can't you control in this situation?

- When would you like to meet again to discuss progress?

- How can we stay on track with this plan?

Evaluating: This stage is where you reflect together at the beginning **of the subsequent coaching session** as to whether the coachee acted on the plan you created at the executing stage. If the employee feels like he is being *evaluated* objectively, and this evaluation can highlight real progress, then there is a much greater chance that the coaching sessions will be successful in the long run.

Also, in the evaluation process, the coach and the coachee should always be looking to improve the coaching sessions so they are better both in terms of the process (the actual coaching session) and the outcome (the progress that is made). The coach and the coachee should devote time and energy to reviewing the coaching so that the coaching sessions are always effective. Here are some powerful questions that can drive the discussion in the evaluation phase:

- Did you get time to practice since the last coaching session?

- Do you feel like you're making progress?

- Was the plan we made at the end of the last coaching session realistic?

- Do you feel you are building on your strengths?

- What are you finding frustrating about the coaching sessions?

- How can I be more effective as a coach?

- Are the coaching sessions frequent enough, or too frequent?

- Are there additional resources that you need to help you make progress in the areas we have identified?

Case Study: The Best Coach of All?

So now we know what great coaching sessions look like; first they **engage** the coachee, next they **explore** with the coachee paths that move them forward based on the coaching conversation. The coachee drives these paths. If appropriate, the coach **explains** his perception of the situation, if they believe the coachee is missing an important part of puzzle. A great coaching session also **executes,** in that it has clear outcomes in terms of what needs to happen next. Subsequently an **evaluation** occurs, likely at the next coaching session, so as to monitor progress.

But if we know what great coaching sessions look like, then we also need to know what do great coaches look like? I don't actually mean what they look like in terms of size and shape, but in terms of what their behavior looks like. Okay, I do mean what they look like in size and shape. (Actually, now that I think about it, lots of coaches tend to look the same whether they are a man or a woman—five-foot 10 inches, whistle around the neck, tight shorts, slim, baseball cap, and a big smile.)

In all seriousness, one of the best activities that I do in my coaching workshop (and there are not many great activities, to be fair) is where I get the audience to reflect on what makes a great coach and what makes a bad coach (based on having a coach, in sport, etc.). As I mentioned a few times in this book, some characteristics are always mentioned in this activity. They are: the best coach believes in you, a great coach always turns up, a great coach pushes you outside your comfort zone, a great coach shows you the progress you've made, and they make the coachee feel it's all about them (amongst other less often mentioned things). Bad coaches obviously do the reverse, but as I stated in Chapter 1, they may even do more harm than a great coach does good. With co-author Peter Danaher, we studied[159] the effects of good and bad relationships in a business context and found asymmetric effects—poor relationships had a greater negative effect on overall satisfaction than the positive impact of great relationships.

But what's it like to have a great coach? Well, I spent a day with possibly one of the best coaches in the world, Marius Marginean. He is a ski coaching supervisor at Whistler Blackcomb Ski Resort Company in British Columbia, Canada. Marius now mainly coaches other ski instructors (he observes them conducting lessons and gives them feedback), but he was called into action to coach me. Now, to say Marius is one of the best coaches in the world is obviously a crazy thing to say, and I have no evidence to back it up. But consider this: Whistler Blackcomb is the number one ski resort in North America (as voted continuously by *Ski Magazine* over the years and again in 2016) and Marius is their top coach. See, he must be good!

I don't want to belabor the story ("Too late," you cry!), but I never dreamt I would be writing about Marius in this book. Whistler Blackcomb very kindly donated Marius to me and my wife, Orla, for a day because I had done some work for them. Only after being with Marius for the day did I realize how a great coach *really* operates and that he must be in this book. Obviously, I know after I write this that he will never be available to instruct again!

So what makes Marius great? First, he engages you easily. Marius has been coaching skiing for 20 years at Whistler Blackcomb, but his energy in engaging you is tangible. It's as if it's opening night for him. While he explores your level of skill in the early conversations, he is always in control—he seeks to understand the context of the lesson ("Is this your first day skiing this holiday? First time this season? Are they really the only goggles you have, Mark?"), but he is the expert; he works out what needs to happen next.

When you start skiing he never overwhelms you with advice; over the day he introduced five foundational techniques that build on each other, but he never mentions there are others as he introduces the next—these building blocks are what great coaches do, they have the big picture in their mind and they piece the picture together one part at a time. Of course, Marius has to deviate at times as things don't go according to plan ("Mark it is better if your head is out of the snow" and "Mark let's get you dressed properly"—okay, so the first one is not true, but the second one is—my ski socks were not pulled up at the beginning and were restricting my foot movement, and he even spotted that, embarrassing). Great coaching relationships never run a smooth course.

The pace is perfect, as Marius knows the pace of the lesson is key to a great experience. But here is the thing, Marius slows the coaching session down, he doesn't speed it up. He forces us to stop and enjoy the view. He knows if we get tired, we stop learning, and skiers have accidents when they are exhausted.

Marius's line is: "Who is the best skier on the mountain, Orla?"

Orla gulps. "Er, you?"

"No! The one who is having the most fun." Coaching is about being in the moment and is as much about relationships as the learning. Learning is social and that's why relationships are so important. Learning doesn't happen without a connection to the coach and given that, unlike my time with Marius, the coaching relationship often endures many months or even years, this connection is key.

Another huge part of what Marius does is the self-belief or the "Woof!" Faced with a tough green run, he tells us to shout, "Woof!" before we head down. Being tentative will cause us more problems. "Be confident, you can do this, attack it, say woof!"

"WOOF!" Orla and I say, and Orla pushes me face down in the snow and heads off. It works! As I stated earlier in this book, great coaches are psychologists by no small feat; reading you, building you up, believing in you, helping you find the way forward. The mental part is so absolutely key in coaching.

Of course, Marius spends most of his time demonstrating what we need to learn and then observing us, but could we observe ourselves? Marius pulls off a great trick; he asks for my phone and tells us to head off down the mountain—will he disappear with my iPhone 12? No. He lets us go, and then starts filming us, and then catches up to us, keeps recording, and flies past us (he IS stealing it!), then he stops at the bottom of the hill and films us coming toward him. The end product is amazing, a great memory and learning tool as well—we see the things we are doing well—and the things we are doing badly. Just like Delta Dental and Joey Restaurant Group, great coaching organizations and coaches are always looking to innovate and keep the momentum going.

As my wife says, "Marius made me want to ski more," and that's what great coaches do. They make you want more coaching, desire more feedback, and build motivation.

The story doesn't quite end there. A few days later when I'm on the mountain again, I get a call. It's Marius. He has just finished coaching another instructor and he has an hour free. Are we on Blackcomb, could we meet? He wants to check in with us (the final tight in action). We meet outside the Rendezvous lodge, and we head off to 7th Heaven. This time we have our three kids with us, so Marius helps them, too, and focuses on Kian who is 10 and needs a little more help with his parallel turns. We are doing our final run with Marius when we stop a third of the way down the mountain, and he says he has to go—he has a meeting in 10 minutes at the bottom of the hill (really 10 minutes!). He turns to Kian and says, "And what's the most important thing to remember, Kian?"

"To turn in parallel?" he replies.

"NO!" Marius fires back at him. "To have fun, WOOF!" he cries and off he disappears down the mountain.

Coaching Checklists

What follows is a coaching checklist that can be used to ensure that you are always doing the right things in terms of managing the coaching sessions to ensure long-term success. Checklists are everything! If you have not read *The Checklist Manifesto*,[160] you're crazy!

There are two case studies at the end of this chapter, which I wrote just for you. Use them to practice the fair process model. I have completed one for you, but the other one is your chance to practice. Obviously, you can then use these case studies in your organization to demonstrate to your coaches how to best use the fair process model.

The last chapter, if you're still awake, relates to the evaluation phase of the fair process model. How do you know your coaching is making a difference? If you can't measure the success of your coaching, then there always will be a nagging voice in the back of your head wondering whether coaching is a good use of your time.

Coaching Checklist

Annual reviews with employees will be easy with regular coaching. On-going documentation is easy to assemble into other documents and demonstrate alignment with the firm's leadership values.

After the coaching session, ask yourself:

Immediately

- Did I encourage self-direction? (Autonomy)

- Did I activate fair process?

- Did I support skill development (technical or values based)? (Mastery)

- Did I demonstrate how this staff person contributes to the firm's vision or connect this coaching session to their goals/career? (Purpose)

Continuously

- Check for progress.

- Document progress (see Chapter 8).

- Praise progress.

- Continue to coach—it can often take months for a new behavior to become habit.

- Listen for feedback. How is the employee coping with the change/project/growth? Can you help by removing obstacles, giving encouragement, enlisting additional assistance?

- Make modifications to the action plan if necessary.

Annual (Semi-Annual or Quarterly) Review

- Review goals—tie-in to the firm's values, strategic priorities, etc.

- Check for progress.

- Review documentation—update as necessary.

- Praise progress.

- Share observations.

- Collaborate to develop new goals—ensure tie-in to firm values/ strategies.

Practice Case 1
Coaching New Guest Service Recruits at a Ski Resort

Janet Davis opened her calendar and realized she was scheduled to meet Jack Deer, a new recruit from Auckland, New Zealand, who she had observed in his new role in guest services. Janet had observed him for 20 minutes with six customers. Although he did a good job, he certainly had some areas to grow in. It was early in the ski season and this was a good time to coach, as the queues were not as long as they would be in a few weeks, and it was not possible to do all training in advance; some things had to be learned on-the-job.

In terms of *reliability*, she had seen that returning guests were confused and a little frustrated (and Jack, too) as he was not necessarily 100 percent confident in the products and services the ski resort offered. In one case, the customer had told Jack what to do. When Jack was dealing with a straightforward inquiry, you could see his personality shine and his confidence quickly develop. However, with a slightly more complex inquiry he looked like a deer caught in the headlights.

In terms of *responsiveness*, Jack was excellent at showing his willingness to help. In one case he proactively suggested a better lift pass to customers than the one they were thinking of buying—based on asking them about their skiing plans for the year. However, his speed and efficiency were, not surprisingly, weak. At one point Janet saw a customer blow his cheeks out and look at his watch as Jack tried to execute a transaction in the system.

In terms of *building relationships*, Jack was outstanding. As noted above, when things were going smoothly Jack was very good at looking a customer in the eye and asking them about their plans for the day. He also had joked with one Australian skier that he hoped he had a better time on the slopes than their team did in the last Rugby World Cup final. However, when things got complex Jack went into his shell and made the whole transaction even worse by ignoring the customer and almost pretending they were not there.

When Janet went back to her notes, she also noted that Jack was awesome at greeting the customer. He started the conversation warmly, but generally let the customer go without even a "goodbye" as he looked toward the next customer in the lineup. To a certain extent, this meant that some of the good work done in building a relationship early on was lost, as the customer may have felt that Jack was simply going through the motions rather than authentically personalizing the experience.

Janet shut her computer down, picked up her coaching checklist and playbook, and prepared to meet Jack. She knew that these early coaching sessions were critical in terms of motivating Jack and getting the ski resort's service philosophy across. She wanted him to feel empowered and that this was not remedial coaching. To ensure this, she zeroed in on the notion that he must pick up most of the opportunities for improvement himself, not by her downloading ideas onto him. There was a knock at the door and Janet saw Jack through the window.

Here is an example of how you could use "fair process" in this case.

Engage: Janet must set the context. She could frame it to highlight that everyone can grow in customer service skills and the ski resort's job is to help Jack become better at serving customers, and that these are skills he can take with him into any job once the ski season ended. Also, Janet should keep in mind autonomy, mastery, and purpose in setting the context. Janet should think about enabling Jack to bring out his personality in the transaction and also encourage Jack to spot improvements for himself (autonomy), that even the very best service providers, with much experience, can grow their skills (mastery), and that the ski resort's number one strategic priority is to deliver service excellence (sense of purpose).

Explore: There is a great chance that Jack will pick up on quite a few pieces, in terms of what he felt he did well, what was tricky for him, and what he could do differently. He's obviously going to pick up on his difficulty in executing some of the transactions and likely to pick up on his strong ability to build rapport with customers. It would be interesting to see if Jack picked up on how he goes into his shell when things get difficult, but it is unlikely he'll realize that he lets the ending of the conversation drift as the customer leaves.

Explain: Given that Jack has picked up a lot about how he can improve, etc., it is now the coach's job to positively reinforce the things that Jack is doing well, whether he's picked up on them or not. Reminding Jack that his bubbly personality is winning over customers will provide an extra spring in his step. Also, congratulating him on advising the customer on a better lift pass, thereby customizing the transaction toward them, would be a great way to reinforce the importance of having the right product knowledge. Identifying some of the things that Jack can improve on, if he has missed them, would also be useful for him—such as giving away the ending of the conversations and finding some of the more technical parts of this job tricky. Again, the important part here is that this is NOT remedial coaching, but that Jack clearly needs some training in some parts of this job, and identifying these so he can get better and better.

Execute: This part is the most important. What does Jack need to improve on to plug his ability gaps, so he can deliver an outstanding experience every time? Does he need some technical training? Does he need to spend some time side-by-side with someone who is a lot more of an expert in some of these areas? Does he simply need to ask more questions when he gets stuck (to the manager perhaps), and is this a confidence issue? Clearly articulating a plan and getting Jack to commit to it is the idea of the execute part of fair process. The more Jack creates the plan and commits to the plan, the fairer the process is.

Evaluate: Obviously the evaluate part comes in the next coaching session, where Janet examines whether Jack has gotten any better in some of these transactions. As long as Jack has executed on the plan, it is very likely that his performance would have improved. When Janet identifies this at the end of a coaching session and praises him on his progress, it becomes a very powerful moment for Janet and Jack.

A great way to use this case is to get two people in the room to buddy up with each other; one acts as Jack and the other acts as Janet, and they practice this case as the coach and the coachee. Once it has been practiced and once it works really well, then get them to sit down and reflect on how they could be a better coach (maybe for about five minutes). Then have them to do the exercise again so they get to practice as a coach for a second time. They do this by walking across the room and finding someone who has played Jack in the previous round with another coach.

While coaching, I also ask the coaches to do anonymous electronic voting to say how they felt they improved from the first to the second time—usually about 80 percent say they felt they were a lot better second time round. This instant gratification gives them much confidence in using the coaching model.

The person who was the coachee (Jack), now acts as the coach for the case below (Keith) and the person who was the coach, now plays the coachee (Erin). Rinse and repeat as above. In this way, both people get to play coach and coachee twice in an exercise that lasts about 45 minutes.

Practice Case 2
Coaching Food Servers

Keith Valley picked up his new mystery shopping report. Each day Keith would receive a new mystery shopping case based on one of the servers in one of his three restaurants in Seattle. In this case it was a server in the Kitson Bar & Grill, which was a popular tourist and locals spot, particularly in the spring and summer when the outdoor patio got busy. The mystery shop was, essentially, observational coaching data. Even though it wasn't Keith himself who had done the observation, the mystery shop acted as an excellent surrogate, as it was very detailed and based on one server only—so it was possible to zero in on their performance alone.

The new server, Erin, had some experience serving in bars, but this was a completely different environment with different clientele. These were not crusty old men who came into the bar, but a younger, more affluent clientele whose expectations were slightly higher.

Unfortunately, the mystery shop was not very flattering. Erin had scored poorly on "expertise" in being able to describe items on the menu and even worse on number of errors she had committed. Erin had made mistakes, but had not picked up on them until the customer had pointed them out. In one case it was an additional food item that was on the bill that should not have been there. Erin had done a very good job recovering from these errors, but the mystery shopper had noted that these may have been unacceptable by more demanding clientele.

The mystery shopper also had noted that Erin had made little effort to personalize the experience toward them, although she noted that Erin's parting conversation was both funny and engaging. However, there was very little in terms of conversation at the beginning or the middle of the experience.

Erin had excelled at "efficiency." She was attentive to the table, and the meals and drinks had always come in an appropriate amount of time. This was generally typical in February when things were slow, but she might be stretched to be as efficient as they got busier in the spring and summer. The mystery shopper had noted that generally Erin had an air of calm about her and seemed very organized.

Certainly Keith felt, when reading the mystery shopper report, that her lack of warmth early on in the experience may make longer wait times harder for the customer to take. Also with the restaurant's goal of being world-class in customer service, the personalization piece was critical.

Another area for opportunity for Erin is taking ownership. The mystery shopper had deliberately asked Erin questions about the best places to visit in Seattle (the shopper acted as if she was a tourist there) and Erin said she really didn't spend a lot of time in the city, so she couldn't help—Keith thought she could have made a much bigger effort to ask other servers in the restaurant for some suggestions.

Given the disheartening mystery shopping report, Keith was not sure how to tackle this coaching session with Erin. He had personally interviewed Erin before she was hired and was pretty sure she was made of the right stuff. He thought about his best sports coaches and how they had helped him, and remembered the advice he got in his coaching training course: The best coaches believe in their athletes, and that's exactly what he needed to do for Erin. He decided to focus on the positive aspects of the mystery shop and use the areas of weakness as ways for Erin to grow by reminding her that the best servers got the best gratuities and were loved by customers. Critically, he must ensure that the mystery shop was only used for formative feedback and not summative feedback.

Keith opened his computer and sent Erin an email asking her to come for a coaching session with him—all employees were told when they were hired that they would have ongoing coaching sessions with team leaders, so this meeting would be no surprise. He wrote the email and sent the appointment, and before he even sat back in his chair and wondered how we would handle the coaching conversation, Erin's accepted invite was back in his mailbox. Responsiveness, he realized, was clearly Erin's strongest asset.

Your turn: (I did the last one for you for goodness sake). This one is a little bit harder; as it may be hard for Erin to remember which customer this was, so the explore part could be tricky. Probably the best approach would be to ask Erin about how she believes she could grow rather than trying to remember this one particular customer.

Engage:

Explore:

Explain:

Execute:

Evaluate:

Moment of Power 8:
The Moment You Measure the Success of Your Coaching

"In God we trust; all others must bring data."
W. Edwards Deming

Have you seen *Moneyball*? Great movie, isn't it? Many people say Brad Pitt looks just like me. But compared to me, I think he's pretty ugly (see photo inside).

The interesting bit about *Moneyball*, of course, is the use of statistics to assist in athletic success. The movie is about moving away from intuition and gut reaction, to using statistics and measurements as the mechanics of success. It is also about smashing a small ball with a big stick, which is less interesting, if you ask me.

Anyway, that sums up the approach to this book and chapter. We can't rely on gut reaction and intuition to tell us whether coaching is going to be a success or not. Coaching is far more important than that. If we don't measure the success of coaching, we cannot tell the difference between effective coaching and ineffective coaching. If we don't measure the success of coaching, the leaders of the organization might start to question whether it's a good use of our time. If we don't measure the success of coaching, then we cannot continuously improve our coaching by getting feedback on it.

This chapter looks at:

- Coaching in the context of *process excellence*

- How to measure the effectiveness of coaching

- How to apply Kirkpatrick's four levels of evaluation to coaching

- The need to apply the results of empirical assessments of coaching effectiveness to improve coaching methods and approaches

Process Excellence

Hands down, the best course I have ever participated in was the principles of process excellence course I did at Commonwealth Bank. The instructors were amazing. They made all the learning game-like so that the material was easy to remember and digest. Even though I did this class in 2008, I still remember all of the key principles, which have influenced me in writing this book.

To start, I would like to cast your mind back to The American Family Insurance case in Chapter 2. It used a lean methodology (which is essentially a process excellence methodology) to drive its coaching forward. Coaching, simultaneously, then helped them execute their lean approach. This section of the book builds on that notion.

One principle of process excellence that is relevant revolves around measurement. Process excellence methodology uses measurement to establish baselines to understand if change has occurred, uses measurement to communicate what is important throughout the organization, and uses measurement to help shape behaviors—people change their behaviors based on what gets measured and rewarded.

The same must be true for coaching—if we don't establish measures for a baseline, and if we don't measure coaching performance using metrics, it's really hard to understand if we are continuously improving through coaching (both the coachee's performance and the coaching process itself). In process excellence, decisions are driven by data not intuition and the same must be true for coaching. Any decision that will impact the coaching process should be made using data.

The key, therefore, is to determine the metrics that are most relevant to the coaching process performance. We must ensure that measures will encourage the right behaviors from both the coach and the coachee. Where possible, these metrics should be linked to the team and individual KPIs (key performance indicators). This relates back to building a system for coaching—if coaching measurements are related to leaders' KPIs then coaching will be taken more seriously across the organization.

Another principle of process excellence is that you must coach people for performance excellence. In the context of process excellence, regular coaching is seen as a way to help people be more effective in completing work. Coaching drives self-sustaining and enduring change and helps people reach their potential. Coaching reinforces the contribution each person makes to achieve the required process and outcomes.

In process excellence, not surprisingly, coaching that is based around observation and process performance data is advocated. Performance improvement targets from coaching should be measurable and regularly reviewed to ensure they are relevant and achievable. This highlights the need for clear and specific learning outcomes from the coaching sessions.

There are three separate but related points here: 1) coaching drives a continuous improvement culture. By constantly coaching people, they see progress and want more of it; 2) in a process excellence culture everyone gets coached, as regular coaching helps people to be more effective irrespective of whether they are poor or strong performers; 3) we must also use the continuous improvement approach to assess the capability of coaches to coach and provide ongoing development and education to improve their skill as a coach—this was part of the coaching system we highlighted in Chapter 2.

How to Measure the Effectiveness of Coaching

Organizations are always looking at their training programs with an eye toward understanding the effects of these programs on the development of their employees. We also know that we need measurable models to analyze our coaching program. This allows us to bypass *winging it* coaching in support of using systems that are designed to achieve tangible and measurable results as process excellence would always encourage us to do.

Building your coaching program and establishing benchmarks against which to measure the coaching program is much easier when you use a recognized learning model with a proven record of accomplishment. When looking to achieve measurable results that can lead to increased performance for your coaches and coachees, Donald Kirkpatrick (2009)[161] created a model for evaluating the success of training programs that is well respected and used all over the world.

But before Donald, let's do the last random story—yippee!

Random Story #8: Measurement Madness

Of course, in terms of measurement, the most annoying piece of measurement, ever, is the customer satisfaction survey or the opinion surveys we are asked to fill out when someone stops us on the street. How fast are we prepared to run to get to the other side of the street if you see someone approaching you with a clipboard? Personally, I'm willing to risk death to get the other side of the road before they reach me. Also, if I do get caught, the research they ask me to do is often useless. For example, someone stopped me the other day and said, "Could you spend five minutes helping me with global warming research?"

I said, "Sure, but we're not going to get much done in five minutes, I think it's going to take a lot longer to crack that one."

What I find really annoying about the customer satisfaction survey is that the survey collector always, incredibly, underestimates the amount of time it's going to take fill out the survey, so they don't put you off at the beginning. They say, "Would you mind filling out the survey? It will take no more than 10 minutes." Three days later you're still there answering questions on the cleanliness of the fingernails of the person who served you last Tuesday.

Equally as annoying as the market research phone calls we get at home are the phone calls we get asking for donations to random charities that we often have never heard of. Out of all the stories that I've heard in the workshops I have taught, the following story is, by far, the best story I have heard. The story came from a participant in the audience when I was asking for customer service stories.

So, the lady who told the story said she was sitting at home in the evening and there was a phone call from a charity collecting for sick children. They asked her to donate some money after they explained the purpose of the charity. This lady went silent as she thought about whether she should make a donation or not, given that she already contributed to a lot of charities recently.

As this lady went silent, the call center employee turned to his friend in the next cubicle, thinking the silence meant she had put the phone down, and said, "The fat cow put the phone down on me." Now, because she was still on the phone—having only gone silent—she was outraged. But before she could say anything, the employee hung up on her (because he thought she had already hung up). The next bit is brilliant. This lady remembered the name of the charity and quickly Googled the number, shaking with fury. After speaking to a number of people at the charity, she finally got through to the employee's supervisor and explained the whole story and told the supervisor how furious she was (she also said, in fact, she wasn't fat and she actually looked quite good). The supervisor, who was a woman, listened very carefully and then finally said, "I can't believe that happened. I don't know what he was thinking; he should have put you on mute when he said it." Certainly, a coaching opportunity for both the supervisor and employee.

If you have a better story, please send it to me!

The Kirkpatrick Model

The Kirkpatrick model, which is arguably the premier model for affecting good learning outcomes, was devised in the 1950s. This model outlines a four-level evaluation model for instructional programs. In terms of a coaching program, the four levels would look like this:

- Reaction—how much do coachees like the coaching process?

- Learning—what did the coachees learn from coaching?

- Behavior—what were the changes in the coachees' behavior because of the coaching?

- Results—what are the tangible benefits of the coaching program?

The model seeks to draw out actionable information on the effectiveness of any coaching program in the hopes of gathering formative feedback to improve the program. It's an ideal framework from which to structure coaching that will capture most of the successful outcomes we are looking for—did the coachee engage with the program, did they learn from the coaching, did they change their behaviors based on the feedback they received in the coaching program, and were there tangible results from the coaching program (more productivity, higher customer satisfaction, etc.)? This model works best because it fits perfectly with the process excellence approach that we identified above. We must create measurements that we get from coaching to ensure both the coaching process and the coachee are improving continually—and this model enables us to achieve that.

The Kirkpatrick Assessment

We now take a detailed look into the components of the four assessment levels; Kirkpatrick's four levels of evaluation offer a clear structure to determine the effectiveness of your coaching program to achieve its learning outcomes.

Level One: Reaction

The first level looks at coachees' reactions to the coach, the coaching sessions, and the coaching program. Typically collected from a questionnaire, the questions solicit the coachees' reaction regarding whether they are motivated and inspired by the coaching sessions and recommendations for improvement.

The advantages are numerous. You will know how the participants felt about the coaching, it will tell you how engaged the participants were with the coaching, and you will come away with a detailed, level one evaluation that can provide critical formative evaluation information that can be used to improve future coaching sessions. This survey can be very simple (please go to our website to view an example).

Level Two: Learning

Level two evaluation questions seek to measure the degree to which coachees have absorbed the coaching, to see if there has been a change in knowledge, skill, and attitudes—before and after coaching (where, if possible, we can use a control group[162] to compare changes). To be able to evaluate successfully the learning that occurred, there must be clearly stated learning objectives at the outset of the coaching sessions in terms of what the goals of the coaching sessions are; where you and the coachee agree they can grow and the skills and knowledge you will specifically focus on. Without these clear learning objectives it is far more difficult to measure successful learning outcomes.

Knowledge is typically measured using already available or coach-constructed *achievement tests* (i.e., tests designed to measure the degree of learning that has taken place). An example of this could be where you have coached an employee on a particular process. For example, after implementing a quality assurance process over a number of weeks, you want to run an achievement test to see if the employee fully understands that process. The achievement test might examine how well the coachee understands each step of the quality assurance process, as well as knowledge-based questions on the technical aspects of the quality assurance process. Skill is typically measured through *performance tests*. For example, if the learning objective was to learn how to make effective presentations, the coachees would need to be evaluated on actual presentations that they subsequently give.

Attitudes to learning are measured with questionnaires similar to the questionnaires described for a level one evaluation. In this case the attitudes and perceptions should be both coach and coachee data (did the coach see learning, did the coachee feel like he had learned?). An example of a coach's assessment survey is included online.

There are many advantages of measuring level two outcomes. First, demonstrating that the coachees are learning will help coaches persuade others that coaching is working and is a worthwhile exercise. Knowledge of level two evaluations can also help in interpreting the results from the level three evaluations (e.g., if level three results do not occur—level three changes are actual behavior changes—it may be because of workplace factors and not because of any flaw in the coaching). Finally, detailed level two evaluation can provide formative information that can be used to improve future versions of the coaching (e.g., you may find specific learning objectives that are rarely being met).

Level Three: Behavior Changes

The third level looks to see what effects training has had on coachee behavioral changes. Therefore, a level three evaluation will follow the coachee's progress, post-coaching, to see if the coaching conversations have been applied to his work. Here, your goal is to find out if coaching program participants have changed their behavior as a result of having attended and participated in the coaching. If the behavior change does not occur, you will want to find out why the change did not occur. The key level three question is: Did the training have a positive effect on job performance? Level three evaluation specifically involves measuring the transfer of knowledge, skills, and attitudes from the training context to the workplace.

There are many advantages of level three evaluations. First, they provide measurement of actual behavior on the job, rather than only measuring or demonstrating positive reaction and/or learning. This is important because you want to have real changes occur from the coaching program. Level three outcomes are required for level four outcomes (i.e., they are the intervening variables or factors that lead to level four outcomes). Most level three outcomes are inherently useful, even if level four outcomes (i.e., business results) are never fully demonstrated. For example, in many situations, evidence of level one outcomes, level two outcomes, and level three outcomes will be adequate evidence of the merit and usefulness of coaching. This is especially true when *all* of these provide evidence of positive results of the coaching.

Level Four: Evaluation of Training

A level four evaluation of coaching is aimed at identifying tangible results from coaching programs, usually in the longer-term. The evaluation process asks whether the coaching increased productivity or profits, reduced costs, increased employee retention, or created higher morale.

Here are some examples of different kinds of level four outcomes:

- Improved quality of work

- Higher productivity

- Reduction in turnover

- Increased sales

- Lower absenteeism

- Higher employee engagement

- More innovation

- Higher customer loyalty

- Higher profits

Level four evaluation is difficult in the sense that it is challenging to establish definite evidence that a coaching program was the key or only the source that produced the level four outcomes. Many other factors may also occur during the coaching period, such as a change in organizational fortunes, coachee health, other team members joining or leaving, etc. How do we know which factors actually played a substantive role? It is hard to isolate the effect of coaching because there are usually many additional causal variables operating on the level four outcome variables (i.e., the coaching event is just one of many potential causes).

For example, let's say you coach for the first time 12 customer service teams in a call center over three months. It was not possible to do a control group, as leadership felt it would be unethical to coach some teams and not others, so they use pre- and post-customer satisfaction surveys to ascertain the results of coaching. How do you know it was the coaching that led to an increase in the results? Could it be the Hawthorne Effect[163] (we just gave the customer service teams some attention!), or a new, successful product that was launched during the experimentation period? Or maybe new employees were added to teams, so it gave each employee more time with customers, etc.

It might seem a bit bizarre that I am advocating for level four analysis and now I'm saying the results could be spurious. The point, simply, is to be careful of the attributions you make when evaluating level four results, we often make causal attributions that don't exist.

Again, the analogy with an athletic team is a good one. To what extent can we explain the results of an athletic team solely down to coaching in a season?

Players could leave, players could join, and players could get injured. Your team may be placed in a weak or strong competitive set. Your team may have a particularly weak or strong team that particular year, etc. Of course, coaching *will* make a difference—we know this to be true. But you just cannot say it makes the *only* difference, so we must be careful interpreting results.

Kirkpatrick (2009) has three main recommendations for level four. First, use the strongest experimental design that is feasible. Second, repeat the measurement at appropriate times. (Repeated measurement can provide data on the long-term pattern of results.) Finally, allow time for results to be achieved. In other words, many level four outcomes will take some time to occur.[164]

Below is a summary of levels one to four with brief descriptions and the characteristics of the evaluation, examples of evaluation tools, and methods for each level and their relevance and practicality. This is a useful summary sheet to remind you what you need to collect at each level.

Summary of the Four Levels of Coaching*

Level	Evaluation type (what is measured)	Evaluation description and characteristics	Examples of evaluation tools and methods	Relevance and practicality
1	Reaction	How the coachee felt about the coaching experience	- Verbal responses - Post-training surveys or question-naires (see example in Appendix)	- Quick and very easy to obtain - Not expensive to gather or to analyze - Opportunity to change to meet the needs of the coachee - Looking for formative feedback to improve the coaching - Should be anonymous (where possible)
2	Learning	Measurement of the change in knowl-edge, skill and/or attitude—before and after coaching	- Assessment or tests before and after coaching - Interviews, observations, or survey feedback can also be used by coach and coachee	- Clear-cut for quantifiable skills - Less easy for complex learning - Be sure to benchmark and check for progress over time
3	Behavior	Extent of applied learn-ing back on the job (implementation)	- Observation and interview over time are required to assess change, relevance of change, and sustainability of change	- Measurement of behavior change typically requires observation over a period of time - Can be done by peers or supervisors
4	Results	Effect on the business or environment by the coachee	- Measures are already in place via normal management systems and reporting (360 degree feed-back etc.) - Higher productivity	- Individually not difficult; more challenging for the whole organization - Process must attribute clear accountabilities and tie them to organizational goals and objectives - Very hard to determine causality

*Adapted from the Kirkpatrick Learning Model

Case Study:
Reading Together® program in New Zealand

There are three reasons I like this last case study. First, this is a completely different coaching context than any of the other cases that I have presented so far, and is a great reminder that coaching comes in all shapes and sizes. The coaching in *Reading Together®* is multi-layered, occurring in (a) published resources, an online Support Desk, and (where possible) briefing meetings for teachers and librarians, (b) workshops with 12-15 parents, and (c) homes with children. This case study focuses only on the workshops for parents. As you'll see below, a strong athletic approach to coaching occurs within these workshops. In this respect, it is also a group-coaching example (as are the briefing meetings).

The second reason I like this case study is because it brings in so many elements of the book. Taking a systems approach to coaching, taking an athletic approach to coaching, and, most importantly, using measurement and feedback to show the impact of coaching are all integral processes of *Reading Together.*®

The third reason I like this case study is that it reminds us that coaching can be used just as appropriately in the non-profit context as in a for-profit context. Educational institutions can use coaching just as much as any other organization and this is a great example of how you can do it.

Reading is an area of learning that all parents recognize as being important, and many well-intentioned parents endeavor to help their children with reading at home. However, parental "help" can often be unsound, unhelpful, and even harmful: the impact on children's reading development can inadvertently be negative rather than positive. *Reading Together®* is a research-based workshop program which addresses this issue. The program, which has been successfully implemented by teachers in New Zealand since 1982, complements and supports school language and literacy programs.

The primary purpose of the *Reading Together®* program is to help all children become keen, competent readers. When implemented as intended, *Reading Together®* enables parents to provide informed and effective support for their children's reading. As a result, experiences with reading at home become positive and mutually enjoyable, rather than stressful and frustrating for both children and adults alike. The program comprises (a) four workshops, each of an hour and a quarter, over seven weeks (that is, a total of five hours workshop time), (b) resources for parents and families, and (c) a fully-scripted Handbook for Workshop Leaders.

Reading Together® is a practical, user-friendly, and manageable program for teachers, librarians, and diverse parents and children. The program is grounded in the realities of participants' lives, and is carefully designed to empower teachers, parents, and librarians to work together in informed, collaborative, and mutually respectful ways. *Reading Together®* recognizes and values the experiences and expertise that each participant brings, and it enables successful coaching and reciprocal learning to occur within contexts which are meaningful, enjoyable, and non-threatening for all participants.

Systems approach—the system *Reading Together®* has created has been so successful that already more than 30,000 parents in New Zealand (total population 4.5 million) have participated in this program (wow!). It is implemented in collaboration with community libraries, so that the librarians understand what the program is trying to achieve and actively support the families and schools involved; for example, by helping parents and children access appropriate resources to read together at home during and beyond the workshops. In the first workshop, the library representative talks about how the library can help them (the parents) and encourages them to visit the library with their children. Where possible, the last workshop is held in the library so that parents can borrow resources and become more confident in the library environment.

The *Reading Together®* workshops are led by competent, experienced teachers who volunteer to implement the program as *part* of the educational system, usually in their own schools and with the support of their school leaders—not on their own.

Observational and demonstration based—this program has all the elements of an athletic-based approach to coaching. For example, during Workshop One, the suggestions for helping with reading at home are demonstrated live with a child who is part of the workshop (rather than playing a video of a child reading). These live demonstrations are much more meaningful, useful, and compelling than a video recording of a child reading with an adult. The suggestions are then practiced at home and during the workshops.

Children participate in Workshop Two with their parents, and spend time selecting appealing and manageable resources, which they then enjoy reading together—with low key, unobtrusive encouragement and support from the Workshop Leader(s).

Measurement based—Workshop Leaders systematically gather data from parents, children, librarians, and classroom teachers about the qualitative and affective outcomes of *Reading Together,*® as well as changes in children's reading achievement. This feedback (gathered during the setting up and implementation of the workshop series) provides useful information about the changes that occur in (a) interactions and relationships around reading, and (b) engagement and enjoyment of reading. These are among the significant and valued outcomes of *Reading Together*® that are critical to sustained gains in children's reading achievement—gains which are one of the ultimate aims of the program.

They actually have demonstrated an impact on children's reading ability through a research study, which was both action research and experimental—it included a randomized, controlled trial.

Below I highlight how they collect information on each level of the Kirkpatrick Evaluation model.

Level One: Reaction

In terms of the reaction to the workshops, at the end of each series of workshops, a brief report by the Workshop Leader is written based on the feedback they received from parents throughout the program about what worked well and what didn't work well. This after-action review, for themselves and other Workshop Leaders, enables them to consider what changes, if any, they need to make when they are implementing their next series of workshops.

Level Two: Learning

Level two evaluation questions measure the degree to which coachees have absorbed the coaching, to see if there has been an increase in knowledge or skill. In this case, Workshop Leaders collect the data, through post-hoc surveys, as to the extent to which parents have understood and effectively utilized the key concepts and helping strategies, which have been explained, demonstrated, and practiced throughout the workshop program.

Level Three: Behavior Changes

In level three, through a workshop survey and ongoing informal feedback, they also collect information on (a) changes in attitudes, behaviors, confidence, and relationships (among children and parents), (b) the amount, type, understanding, and difficulty levels of reading undertaken by the children, and (c) use of libraries and resources.

Level Four: Results

Reading Together® research has shown that, when measured against a matched control group, the children whose parents participate in the program make significantly greater gains in reading achievement which are sustained over time. The research also shows that, when Workshop Leaders maintain the fidelity of *Reading Together,*® the program increases children's enjoyment, engagement, independence, and confidence as readers; and improves relationships between children and parents, and between parents and teachers. A great way of demonstrating real results!

Overall, a great case study on a holistic and collaborative approach to coaching in the context of an educational partnership program.

Conclusion

I've said far too much—and yet not enough! Okay, just too much then. It's hard to believe I wrote this in a wet weekend in Nebraska. I hope you are glad it rained (although I could have written it when it was sunny there, too, as there is not much more to do even when the weather is good).

The book closes with a to-do list (below) that you should get to today. Don't procrastinate! Unless, of course, you are reading this in bed before you go to sleep, then it can wait until the morning. I have included online a summary of the eight moments of power and the associated 20 principles that emerge from this book. Happy reading!

I have deliberately kept this book short and silly. A few years ago, I happened to meet my favorite comedian on a plane. After asking him how to become a successful comedian, he said, "There are three rules of great comedy. First, timing. Timing is everything. When you tell the punch line the timing must be exactly right. Second, never give them everything. Always leave them wanting more."

Goodbye.

To-do List

1. How I will adapt my coaching style tomorrow?

2. What do I need to do before coaching to make the coaching a success (align coaching with strategy, ensure buy-in from senior leaders, etc.)?

3. What are the three ways I can coach my team more effectively (technically, mentally, and physically)?

4. How will I take the time to coach my team?

    What will I stop doing (take the time from)?

    Who will I start coaching (take the time for)?

5. What are three ways I can build variety into my coaching (team-based coaching, upward coaching, peer-to-peer coaching, etc.)?

6. How will I ensure that autonomy, mastery, and purpose are present in all coaching sessions? (Clues: start with link to their goals, show progress, empower them to make a plan and own it.)

7. How will I ensure that my coachees and I have a growth mindset?

8. How will I measure the success of my coaching?

Notes

1   http://www.bizjournals.com/boston/news/2011/04/19/survey-major-ity-hate-performance.html

2   Furlow, Bryant. "Tetrodotoxin and the Life Tree." http://dhushara.freehosting.net/book/upd/jun01/20101/tetro.htm

3   Steve Tax from University of Victoria and Ajith Kumar from Arizona State University

4   These coaching practices were, for example, goal-setting, feedback, demonstrating of the skills by the coach, coaching observing employees in their role.

5   See Schaufeli, W.B. & Bakker, A.B. (2004). Job Demands, Job Resources and their Relationship with Burnout and Engagement: A multi-sample study. Journal of Organizational Behavior, 25, 293-315., Xanthopoulou, D., Bakker, A. B., Demerouti, E., & Schaufeli, W. B. (2009). Work Engagement and Financial Returns: A diary study on the role of job and personal resources. Journal of Occupational and Organizational Psychology, 82(1), 183-200., et al. (2009), and Choi, Y. "The differences between work engagement and workaholism, and organizational outcomes: An integrative model." Social Behavior and Personality: an international journal 41.10 (2013): 1655-1665.

6   Latham, G.P., Ford, R.C, Tzabbar, D. (2012). Enhancing Employee and Organizational Performance through Coaching based on Mystery Shopper Feedback: A quasi-experimental study. Human Resources Management, 51(2), 213-230.

7   Elmadağ, A. B., Ellinger, A. E., & Franke, G. R. (2008). Antecedents and consequences of frontline service employee commitment to service quality. Journal of Marketing Theory and Practice, 16(2), 95-110.

8   Latham, G.P., Ford, R.C, Tzabbar, D. ibid

9   Liu, X., & Batt, R. (2010). How Supervisors Influence Performance: A multilevel study of coaching and group management in technology-mediated services. Personnel Psychology, 63, 265-298.

10   Goleman, D. (2000). Leadership that gets results, HBR, March-April 2000, pages 2-15

11   Boyatzis, R. E., Smith, M. L., & Blaize, N. (2006). Developing sustainable leaders through coaching and compassion. Academy of Management Learning & Education, 5(1), 8-24.

12   https://www.youtube.com/watch?v=yVfeezxmYcA&index=2&list=WL

13   Ibid

14   Garvin, D. A. (2013). How Google sold its engineers on management. Harvard Business Review, 91(12), 74-+.

15   (Chartered Institute of Personnel and Development 2012). http://www.cipd.co.uk/binaries/employee-outlook_2012-sprng.pdf

16   Ellinger, A. D., Ellinger, A. E., & Keller, S. B. (2003). Supervisory Coaching Behavior, Employee Satisfaction, and Warehouse Employee Performance: A dyadic perspective in the distribution industry. Human Resource Development Quarterly, 14(4), 435–458. p. 452.

17   Sales Teams Need More (and Better) Coaching, Scott Edinger, 2015 https://hbr.org/2015/05/a-high-percentage-move-to-increase-revenue

18   American Management Association 2008, http://www.pcpionline.com/pdfs/coaching_study_of_successful_practices.pdf

19   Ibarra, H. (2015). Act Like a Leader, Think Like a Leader. Harvard Business Review Press.

20 "Measuring Sales Management's Coaching Impact", 2015, Forum Corp http://salesmanagement.org/web/uploads/pdf/8fa9799a465268 debbc7a352a46b7e94.pdf

21 Silvia, P. J. (2007). How to write a lot: A practical guide to productive academic writing. American Psychological Association.

22 Senge, P. M. (2006). The fifth discipline: The art and practice of the learning organization. Broadway Business.

23 Ibid. p 3.

24 Ibid. p.11

25 Ibid. p.175

26 Ibid. p.12

27 Ibid. p.13

28 Edmondson, A. (1999). Psychological Safety and Learning Behavior in Work Teams. Administrative Science Quarterly, 44(2), 350-383.

29 Duhigg, C. and J. Graham (2016). What Google Learned From Its Quest to Build the Perfect Team, New York Times, Feb. 25.

30 http://www.davidrock.net/files/Driving_Organisational_Change_ with_Internal_Coaching_Programs.pdf

31 https://www.coachingcloud.com/about#for-organisations

32 A huge thanks for CEB for letting us them in this case

33 Kenrick, D. T., & Funder, D. C. (1991). The person-situation debate: Do personality traits really exist? In V. J. Derlega, B. A. Winstead, & W. H. Jones, W. H. (Eds.) Personality: Contemporary Theory and Research (Chapter 6). A commonly used example of person-situation interaction is the Stanford Prison Experiment where college students participated in a study that simulated a prison setting with some students acting as guards and others as prisoners. The study was terminated when the guards became even more abusive than anticipated.

While Philip Zimbardo concluded that the study shows evidence of the effect of the situation transcending personality traits see Haney, C., Banks., C., & Zimbardo, P. (1973). Interpersonal dynamics in a simulated prison. International Journal of Criminology and Penology, 1, 69-97

34   Kahneman, D. (2011). Thinking, Fast and Slow. Macmillan.

35   Ibid. p.23

36   See http://www.beinghuman.org/theme/bias for an excellent summary of the many key ways we are biased

37   Peters, S. (2012). The Chimp Paradox: The Acclaimed Mind Management Programme to Help You Achieve Success, Confidence and Happiness. Random House.

38   In particular Steve Peters is famous for helping the British Olympic team achieve multiple goals in multiple Olympics in helping Ronnie Sullivan become a world championship snooker player again after he was in a career slump.

39   This tendency is called fundamental attribution error

40   Bradley, G. W. (1978). Self-Serving Biases in the Attribution Process: A Reexamination of the Fact or Fiction Question. Journal of Personality and Social Psychology. 36, 56-71. Self-serving bias concept first introduced by Heider, F. The psychology of interpersonal relations. New York: Wiley, 1958.

41   Campbell, W. K., & C. Sedikides(1999). Self-Threat Magnifies the Self-Serving Bias: A Meta-Analytic Integration. Review of General Psychology. 3, 23-43.

42   Amabile, T., & Kramer, S. (2011). The progress principle: Using small wins to ignite joy, engagement, and creativity at work. Harvard Business Press.

43   Hsieh, T. (2010). Delivering happiness: A path to profits, passion, and purpose. Grand Central Publishing.

44   Ibid p.183

45   ibid p.184

46   Hertz H.S., (2011). Director, Baldridge Performance Excellence Program, National Institute of Standards and Technology, 2011, Presentation at the University of Victoria.

47   Blanshard, K. (2016). Critical Leadership Skills: Key Traits That Can Make or Break Today's Leaders http://www.kenblanchard.com/img/pub/pdf_critical_leadership_skills.pdf

48   Ibid

49   Gebhardt, G. F., Carpenter, G. S., & Sherry Jr, J. F. (2006). Creating a market orientation: A longitudinal, multifirm, grounded analysis of cultural transformation. Journal of Marketing, 70(4), 37-55.

50   Hansen, M.T. (2009). "Collaboration: an interview with Morten T. Hansen". http://www.thecollaborationbook.com/hansen.pdf

51   Ibid

52   Ibid

53   Pink, D. H. (2011). Drive: The surprising truth about what motivates us. Penguin.

54   Kanter, R. M. (2013). The happiest people pursue the most difficult problems. Harvard Business Review Blog. Retrieved from http://blogs. hbr. org/2013/04/to-find-happiness-at-work-tap

55   http://deliveringhappiness.com/the-motivation-trifecta-autonomy-mastery-and-purpose/

56   http://deliveringhappiness.com/the-motivation-trifecta-autonomy-mastery-and-purpose/

57   Deci, E. L., & Ryan, R. M. (1985). Intrinsic motivation and self-determination in human behavior. Springer Science & Business Media.

58   https://www.virgin.com/entrepreneur/richard-branson-why-business-is-about-people-people-and-people

59   Pink, D. H. (2011). Drive: The surprising truth about what motivates us. Penguin.

60   Ibid

61   Brown, B., (2012). Presentation at the linkage global Institute for leadership development conference, Palm Desert, CA.

62   Hattie, J. (2013). Visible learning: A synthesis of over 800 meta-analyses relating to achievement. Routledge.

63   Gates, B. (2013) Teachers Need Real Feedback, TED Talk, May.

64   Christensen, S.T. (2015). Three Ways Companies Are Changing The Dreaded Performance Review, Fast Company, October 5th 2015.

65   Stone, D., & Heen, S. (2014). Thanks for the feedback: The science and art of receiving feedback well. Penguin UK.

66   Dweck, C. (2006). Mindset: The new psychology of success. Random House.

67   Hardy, D. (2011). The Compound Effect. Vanguard.

68   Anderman, L. H., & Anderman, E. M. (2009). Oriented toward mastery: Promoting positive motivational goals for students. In R. Gilman, E. S. Huebner, & M. Furlong (Eds.), Handbook of positive psychology in the schools (pp. 161–173). New York, NY: Routledge.

69   Dweck, C. (2006). Mindset: The new psychology of success. Random House.

70   Dweck, C. S., Chiu, C. Y., & Hong, Y. Y. (1995). Implicit theories and their role in judgments and reactions: A word from two perspectives. Psychological Inquiry, 6(4), 267-285.

71   Ibid

72   Dweck, C. (2006). Mindset: The new psychology of success. Random House.

73   Dweck, C. (2006). Mindset: The new psychology of success. Random House.

74   Dweck, C. (2015). Carol Dweck Revisits the "Growth Mindset," Education Week September 22nd

75   Dweck, C. S., Chiu, C. Y., & Hong, Y. Y. (1995). Implicit theories and their role in judgments and reactions: A word from two perspectives. Psychological Inquiry, 6(4), 267-285.

76   Murphy-Paul A., Affirmative Testing Blog: What Students Do With Feedback

77   Kaufman, S. Ungifted: intelligence redefined. Basic Books, 2013.

78   Diagram by Nigel Holmes

79   Heslin, P. A., Vandewalle, D., & Latham, G. P. (2006). Keen To Help? Managers' Implicit Person Theories and Their Subsequent Employee Coaching. Personnel Psychology, 59(4), 871-902 and Vandewalle, D. (2012). A growth and fixed mindset exposition of the value of conceptual clarity. Industrial and Organizational Psychology, 5(3), 301-305.

80   Conger, J., & Toegel, G. (2002). Action learning and multi-rater feedback as leadership development interventions: Popular but poorly deployed. Journal of Change Management, 3(4), 332-348.

81   Heslin, P. A., Latham, G. P., & VandeWalle, D. (2005). The effect of implicit person theory on performance appraisals. Journal of Applied Psychology, 90(5), 842.

82   Heslin, P. A., & VandeWalle, D. (2008). Managers' implicit assumptions about personnel. Current Directions in Psychological Science, 17(3), 219-223. P.219

83   Heslin, P. A., Latham, G. P., & VandeWalle, D. (2005). The effect of implicit person theory on performance appraisals. Journal of Applied Psychology, 90(5), 842.

84   Heslin, P. A., Vandewalle, D., & Latham, G. P. (2006). Keen To Help? Managers' Implicit Person Theories and Their Subsequent Employee Coaching. Personnel Psychology, 59(4), 871-902

85   Stone, D., and S. Heen (2014). Thanks for the feedback: The science and art of receiving feedback well. Penguin.

86   Baker, A., Perreault, D., Reid, A., & Blanchard, C. M. (2013). Feedback and organizations: Feedback is good, feedback-friendly culture is better. Canadian Psychology/Psychologie Canadienne, 54(4), 260.

87   ibid

88   Kang, G. D., Jame, J., & Alexandris, K. (2002). Measurement of internal service quality: application of the SERVQUAL battery to internal service quality. Managing Service Quality: An International Journal, 12(5), 278-291.

89   Parasuraman, A., Berry, L. L., & Zeithaml, V. A. (1991). Refinement and reassessment of the SERVQUAL scale. Journal of Retailing, 67(4), 420.

90   Rhoads, K. V., & Cialdini, R. B. (2002). The business of influence: Principles that lead to success in commercial settings. The Persuasion Handbook, 513-542. (p.525).

91   Foushee, M. C. (1984). Dyads at 35,000 feet: Factors affecting group processes and aircraft performance. American Psychologist, 39, 885-893.

92   See for example Harper, C. R., Kidera, C. J., & Cullen, J. F. (1971). Study of simulated airplane pilot incapacitation. Aerospace Medicine, 42, 946-948.

93   Cialdini, R. B. (2009). Influence: Science and practice (Vol. 4). Boston: Pearson Education.

94   Cialdini, R. B. (2009). Influence: Science and practice (Vol. 4). Boston: Pearson Education.

95   Milgram, S. (1963). "Behavioral study of obedience." Journal of Abnormal and Social Psychology 67: 371–378

96   Heath, C., & Heath, D. (2007). Made to stick: Why some ideas survive and others die. Random House.

97   See for example Langer, E. J., & Saegert, S. (1977). Crowding and cognitive control. Journal of Personality and Social Psychology, 35(3), 175. For a great paper on the use of cognitive control

98   Gladwell, M. (2008). Outliers: The story of success. Hachette UK.

99   Ericsson, K. A., Prietula, M. J., & Cokely, E. T. (2007). The making of an expert. Harvard Business Review, 85(7/8), 114.

100 Ibid p.120

101 Ibid p.120

102 Ibid p.121

103 Ibid p.118

104 Ibid p.121

105 Greenberg, J., & Baron, R. A. (2008). Behavior in organizations. Upper Saddle River, NJ : Pearson/Prentice Hall

106 Stec, D (2009). The Emergence of the Coach and the Arrival of Coaching. Annual Meeting of the Administrative Sciences Association of Canada, Niagara Falls, ON.

107 Read, M.J.B (2011). Investigating organizational coaching through an athletic Coaching comparison: determining high performance coaching practices in organizations. Unpublished PhD Thesis, Vancouver: University of British Columbia

108 Peltier, B. (2001). The Psychology of Executive Coaching: Theory and Application. New York, NY: Brunner-Routledge.

109 Ievleva, L., & Terry, P. C. (2008). Applying sport psychology to business. International Coaching Psychology Review, 3(1), 8-18.

110 Read, M.J.B., Colgate, M., Corwin, V., & Tax, S. (2012). Helping Create Service "Experts": The Opportunity for an Athletic Approach to Coaching in Service Organizations. International Journal of Mentoring and Coaching, 10(1), 24-37.

111 Read, M. J., (2011). Ibid.

112 Read, M.J.B., Colgate, M., Corwin, V., & Tax, S. (2012). Helping Create Service "Experts": The Opportunity for an Athletic Approach to Coaching in Service Organizations. International Journal of Mentoring and Coaching, 10(1), 24-37.

113 Durand-Bush, N., & Salmela, J. H. (2002). The development and maintenance of expert athletic performance: Perceptions of world and Olympic champions. Journal of Applied Sport Psychology, 14(3), 154-171.

114 Becker, A. J. (2009). It's not what they do, it's how they do it: Athlete experiences of great coaching. International Journal of Sports Science & Coaching, 4(1), 93-119.

115 Durand-Bush and Salmela Ibid

116 Durand-Bush and Salmela Ibid p.160

117 Becker Ibid p.108

118 Becker Ibid p.108

119 Durand-Bush and Salmela Ibid

120 Durand-Bush and Salmela Ibid p.165

121 Johnson, S. R., Wojnar, P. J., Price, W. J., Foley, T. J., Moon, J. R., Esposito, E. N., & Cromartie, F. J. (2011). A Coach's Responsibility: Learning How to Prepare Athletes for Peak Performance. The Sport Journal, 14(1), 1.

122 Elberse, A., & Ferguson, A. (2013). Ferguson is a uniquely effective "portfolio manager" of talent. Harvard Business Review, 91(10), 116-125.

123 Ibid p.124

124 Bandura, A. (2000). Exercise of human agency through collective efficacy. Current Directions in Psychological Science, 9(3), 75-78.

125 https://www.youtube.com/watch?v=yVfeezxmYcA&index=2&list =WL if you were a bad person and didn't watch first time around!

126 Read, M. J., (2011). Ibid. p.97

127 Read, M.J.B., Colgate, M., Corwin, V., & Tax, S. (2012). Helping Create Service "Experts": The Opportunity for an Athletic Approach to Coaching in Service Organizations. International Journal of Mentoring and Coaching, 10(1), 24-37. P.30

128 Griffith, C. (2007). Getting Ready to Coach. Essential Readings in Sport and Exercise Psychology, 23-28. P.25.

129 Read, M. J., (2011).

130 Dweck, C. (2006). Mindset: The new psychology of success. Random House.

131 Miner, J. B. (2003). The rated importance, scientific validity, and practical usefulness of organizational behavior theories. Academy of Management Learning and Education, 2, 250–268.

132 Bauer T. and Erdogan B. (2012). An Introduction to Organizational Behavior. Creative Commons.

133 Stein, N. (2000). Measuring people power. Fortune, 142(7), 186. People with difficult goals outperform those with easier goals

134 Latham, G. P., & Locke, E. A. (2006). Enhancing the benefits and overcoming the pitfalls of goal setting. Organizational Dynamics, 35, 332–340.

135 Shaw, K. N. (2004). Changing the goal-setting process at Microsoft. Academy of Management Executive, 18, 139–142

136 Latham, G. P. (2004). The motivational benefits of goal-setting. Academy of Management Executive, 18, 126–129

137 Orlick, T. O. (1990). In Pursuit of Excellence. Human Kinetics, Champaign, Illinois.

138 Vealey, R. S., & Greenleaf, C. A. (2001). Seeing is believing: Understanding and using imagery in sport. Applied sport psychology: Personal growth to peak performance, 4, 247-272.

139 Ibid

140 Peltier, B. (2011). The psychology of executive coaching: Theory and application. Taylor & Francis.

141 Ibid p.177

142 Hardingham, A. (2004). The coach's coach: Personal development for personal developers. CIPD Publishing.

143 Miller, S. L. (2001). The complete player: The psychology of winning hockey. Stoddart Publishing.

144 M.J. Read 2011

145 Ibid

146 Ibid p.101

147 M.J. Read 2011

148 WorkSafeBC, (2009). Worksafe BC Statistics, Annual Report and Service Plan 2009

149 See, for example, Loehr, J., & Schwartz, T. (2001). The Making of a Corporate Athlete. Harvard Business Review, 120-128

150 Evans L, (2103). What 3 Companies Are Doing to Keep Employees Healthy. Entrepreneur, March http://www.entrepreneur.com/article/226041.

151 Ibid

152 Ibid

153 McFarlin, D. B., & Sweeney, P. D. (1992). Research notes. Distributive and procedural justice as predictors of satisfaction with personal and organizational outcomes. Academy of Management Journal, 35(3), 626-637.

154 Lind, E. A., and T. R. Tyler (1988). The social psychology of procedural justice. Springer Science & Business Media.

155 Kim, W. C., & Mauborgne, R. (2003). Fair process: Managing in the knowledge economy. Harvard Business Review, 81(1), 127-136.

156 Adapted from Goodwin, C., & Ross, I. (1992). Consumer responses to service failures: influence of procedural and interactional fairness perceptions. Journal of Business research, 25(2), 149-163.

157 Leventhal, G. S. (1976). Fairness in Social Relationships, General Learning Press, Morristown, NJ.

158 In particular, it is a combination of Kim, W. C., & Mauborgne, R. (2003). Fair process: Managing in the knowledge economy. Harvard Business Review, 81(1), 127-136. And NASA's "The 5E instructional model" http://www.nasa.gov/audience/foreducators/ nasaeclips/5eteachingmodels/ - yes we are even using space research - get ready for takeoff!

159 Colgate, M. R., & Danaher, P. J. (2000). Implementing a customer relationship strategy: The asymmetric impact of poor versus excellent execution. Journal of the Academy of Marketing Science, 28(3), 375-387.

160 Gawande, A. (2010). Checklist Manifesto, The (HB). Penguin Books India.

161 Kirkpatrick, D. L. (2009). Implementing the four levels: A practical guide for effective evaluation of training programs: Easyread Large Edition. ReadHowYouWant.com.

162 A control group is defined as the group in an experiment or study that

does not receive treatment by the researchers and is then used as a benchmark to measure how the other subjects do

163 The Hawthorne effect is where individuals modify or improve an aspect of their behavior in response to their awareness of being observed

164 Kirkpatrick, D. L. (2009). Implementing the four levels: A practical guide for effective evaluation of training programs: Easyread Large Edition. ReadHowYouWant.com.

Index

About the Author

Mark Colgate BSc, Ph.D. is Professor and Associate Dean at the Gustavson School of Business, University of Victoria, Canada. His primary research areas are service excellence and coaching. His research has been published in journals such as *Sloan Management Review, Journal of the Academy of Marketing Science, Journal of Service Research,* and *Journal of Business Research.*

Mark's teaching reflects his research, and as such, he has taught many courses in service excellence and the *8 Moments of Power in Coaching* at undergraduate, postgraduate, and executive levels. He also has taught in China (where he is a regular professor at the China Europe International Business School in Shanghai, the leading business school in China), Australia, New Zealand, and Ireland. Mark has received two university-wide Teaching Excellence Awards. One from the University of Auckland, New Zealand in 1999 and, in 2013, the same award from the University of Victoria, Canada.

Mark recently has returned from three years as the General Manager of Customer Satisfaction at Commonwealth Bank of Australia, the 10th largest bank in the world. He has also consulted for many companies such as Toyota, TELUS, Four Seasons, Whistler Blackcomb, Sony, Schneider Electric, Kiwi Experience Tourism Bus Company, and the BC Government.

elevate
publishing

DELIVERING TRANSFORMATIVE MESSAGES
TO THE WORLD

Visit www.elevatepub.com for our latest offerings.

NO TREES WERE HARMED IN THE MAKING OF THIS BOOK.

OK, so a few did make the ultimate sacrifice.

In order to steward our environment, we are partnered with *Plant With Purpose*, to plant a tree for every tree that paid the price for the printing of this book.

To learn more, visit www.elevatepub.com/about

PLANT WITH PURPOSE | WWW.PLANTWITHPURPOSE.ORG